AutoFellatio

BIOGRAPHY

JAMES MAKER first trod the boards in 1982 as a dancer and backing vocalist with The Smiths, and was erroneously known as "The Fifth Smith".

Later, he became lyricist and lead singer with the 1980s indie group, Raymonde, and 1990s "gay" hard rock group RPLA, releasing the albums *Babelogue* and *Metal Queen Hijack* respectively.

He has appeared in the film *Middleton's Changeling* opposite Ian Dury and Billy Connolly.

In 2004, he supported the New York Dolls on their comeback tour at the Royal Festival Hall in London, and at the Move Festival in Manchester.

In addition to performing spoken word sets, he is currently working on a new satirical work inspired by his time in Spain.

AutoFellatio

JAMES MAKER

hkandescent

INKANDESCENT

Published by Inkandescent, 2017

First published in 2011 by BIGFib Books

A CIP catalogue record for this book
is available from the British Library

Designed by Justin David

Printed in the UK by Severn, Gloucester

MIX
Paper | Supporting
responsible forestry
FSC® C022174

ISBN 978-0-9955346-5-0 (paperback)
ISBN 978-0-9955346-7-4 (Kindle ebook)
ISBN 978-0-9955346-6-7 (Apple iBook)

3 5 7 9 10 8 6 4 2

WWW.INKANDESCENT.CO.UK

CONTENTS

"— Malvadas hermanas, vosotras que atemorizáis
Al viajero solitario por la noche
Que, como lúgubres cuervos gritando
Golpeáis las ventanas del agonizante
Venid! Acudid a mi llamada!
Y compartamos la infamia
De un mal que hará que todo Cartago arda
Acudid! Acudid! — "

Purcell, *Dido and Aeneas*

MY PROVENANCE IS
SOUTH LONDON 60

MY FIRST ACT OF CIVIC VANDALISM wasn't quite like that of other boys. I shinned up a road sign that announced one's arrival in Bermondsey and crayoned it with the travel advisory of Dante's *Inferno*: "Lasciate Ogni Speranza." Abandon All Hope. I had not read Dante but had eagerly swallowed Hubert Selby Jr's *Last Exit To Brooklyn*.

It wasn't a mindless act, but it was rather pointless: in Bermondsey we speak West Indian Patois, Turkish, Amharic and even a dialect of English — but Florentine is thin on the ground. The people of Bermondsey may already have suspected they were living in purgatory, and possibly need not have been reminded of the fact by an alacritous fourteen-year-old.

I am of post-war working class stock and, therefore, designed to receive bad news. In what I like to think of as one of my more charming qualities, I continue to respond to disappointment as if it were an unusual aspect of life. My face is interesting to the degree that my mouth has not yet been disfigured into an inverted moue. That has been a triumph. On a daily basis I have seen constant anticlimax turn other people's mouths inoperably upside down.

I am a commercially unsuccessful singer, although I was an

inner city superstar of unwiped formica, enjoying a moderately lengthy run as the Ava Gardner of SE16.

In 1983, the late and celebrated clairvoyant Doris Stokes, on one of her frequent sorties to the Astral Plane, presented to me as unassailable fact that I am related to the Spanish Armada. I accepted this information, nodding vigorously, which corroborates my instinctive flair for the staccato. I was relieved at not being buried in yet more Wigan. On Planet Earth, my family tree is a rhombus of clogmakers and disinterested fish gutters from Lancashire who moved to London after the Second World War.

Historically a dockers' district, by the time I arrived on the stage Bermondsey was already nosediving towards economic obsolescence amid a utopian experiment of social realism. With the advance of globalisation came the death of old industries, presaging an uncertain future where one's neighbours disappeared and where the streets in which one grew up became an increasingly volatile, Hogarthian rustbelt.

The severity of this depression was such that a Stalinist energy measure was introduced whereby television broadcasting stopped abruptly at 9 o'clock in the evening to encourage the nation to go to bed. Mid-1970s London was really Moscow with John Lewis.

I have always thought that energy was there to be wasted. A relentless flicker of light switches, to my parents' annoyance I would pass from one room to another illuminating the house in broad daylight, until one Thursday, and despite a clear warning, I plugged in a Hoover and was electrocuted. The shock threw me across a downstairs vestibule and into the bathroom.

I never recovered. Electricity. I am at home stationed by a tower of Marshall amplifiers.

As trade swung away from Britain's Commonwealth and towards Europe, the ships that would glide up the Thames like regiments to London's Indian quays dwindled to single spies before vanishing altogether. I remember these modern galleons sailing into Rotherhithe carrying the cargo of rubber, bananas and timber.

Consequently, as the cranes stood idle and the warehouses and wharves lay abandoned, the docks were transformed into a forbidden place of ghost shadows and folk memory.

Immortalised in Charles Dickens' *Oliver Twist*, Rotherhithe docks offered an ideal location in which to be robbed, raped or murdered. Now, in middle age, and driven by the fear of being pauperised by my own longevity, one is tempted to jump into a taxi and head straight there.

Too late, of course. It has reevolved, and today the London docklands once again hum with life. Developers have created a new and sterile zone of glass compounds, air conditioning and expansive coffee tables at which people discuss their investment portfolios in Montecatini.

To revisit the Bermondsey of my youth is also to negotiate stark, overhead lighting. To endure relative poverty and urine-soaked pedestrian underpasses is enough, without additionally being lit from *above*.

A boy emerges, callow, uppish and oversensitive, who clung to dreams in place of experiences and whom cherished fantasy in place of reality. A dubious sense of humour that is not really humour, except perhaps in the sense of "disease", and a devout antipathy towards both mackerel and my surroundings.

Nature abhors a vacuum and bedroom postering soon led to bedroom posturing. A practice deemed to be further proof of a migration towards the suburbs of human existence, I resisted all attempts to navigate me through the portal of a professional life. When asked by the school careers officer what my plans were, I answered, 'I would like to retire.' And I meant it.

I was fourteen in 1975. I remember a sultry August afternoon; the toxic oil drums and the vast echo chamber of an empty warehouse at Greenland Dock. Carried by a zephyr from Millwall, I heard a crystal clear female singing voice; I like to think it was Queenie Watts. Her saeta travelled across the befouled, russet river and that sonorous coda—a concord of dust and memories—filled me with an euphoric sadness. Yearning. Clearly, at that age I was already nostalgic. From that moment, I decided that I wanted to be a singer.

Books were my oxygen, providing escape in the recounting of journeys that I, too, might one day venture. Books are the playmates of those who cannot cut the mustard in the adventure playground of life. But what playmates: Genet, Gide and Swift. Those barbarian epistles of low life mirrored a world that I precociously aspired to lower to. Jean Genet's prose inspired me with its Dionysian, rock star rawness and played a part in eviscerating the last of the boy-child within me. Not difficult.

It took me years to leave the departure lounge of life, and when I arrived at my destination not all my luggage was on the carousel.

A vicinity where brutality was routine, that delta—scorched by football club rivalries, the bouquet of boiled Spam, of creased men with nicotine fingernails and young women of dispensable charms—evinced a topography of casual rage and raucous laughter. Often simultaneously.

But, there existed a generosity and an almost winsome stoicism in its people that is borne of unplanned pregnancies and decades-long deep-fat frying. It wasn't all menial melancholy. Parties were frequent and often disrupted by the arrival of the police. One could always rely upon the curtain up of street theatre, whose First Act opened with:

'Fuck off.'

'No. *You* fuck off.'

That was the birdsong of Southwark.

For people whose ambition is to survive without being sideswiped by the pandemic of margarine, the spiritual world is often an unaffordable resort. The churches of Bermondsey whistled with an empty fairground sinisterness.

One Sunday morning I went to St Andrew's church, long since demolished, and knelt before everything, including its heavy fibre doormat. I felt nothing. Jesus meant nothing to me. Organised religion has made little impact on me because I resent authoritarianism. I think they've had a jolly good run for their money and it's now time for them to *fuck off*, once and for all.

Christened in the Church of England, nevertheless I have been drawn to the architecture of the bespoke cassock, the romance of Mediterranean skin tone and the fresco vividity of Roman Catholicism. It's purely visual: I like the pantone colours and the passion. But we also know that what once might have been attractively olive may turn sallow. Anglicanism, by contrast, is an airless sermon delivered in a draughty basilica by a pederast with a shrill voice and a centre-parting.

My father, an ex-Royal Marine, worked for *The Times* newspaper and my mother worked at the Saint Martin's Theatre where Agatha Christie's *The Mousetrap* still continues to run. They were both hard working and life was a roster of preparing for work when not actually *at* work. My father ceaselessly ironed trousers and polished shoes, ultimately amassing a collection that might have intimidated Imelda Marcos. We maintained an uneasy truce that threatened to tip into hostility at any minute—his hand and my smart-alecky tongue.

My mother was demonstrative in her love for me, although her emotional furniture had been stacked into a corner at my father's infidelities. We always enjoyed an excellent and harmonious relationship.

Now and then, I accompanied my mother to her workplace so that I could wander the theatre before putting my feet up in Marius Goring's dressing room. Marius Goring was a famed British theatre actor of the time who, notably, played the part of Marianne Faithfull's father in *Girl On A Motorcycle*. A box of greasepaint, a bottle of cognac and a girdle thrown over the back of a fauteuil; a lightbulbed mirror decoratively studded with exclamatory telegrams from Trieste and New York. The allure of the dressing room, and its vapours, are lethal. I knew it was for me.

I did love my father, but never moreso than after he died. That is to say that I did not realise how much I loved him until after his death. When my father died of cancer in the June of 1995, I felt an inappropriate and inexplicable excitement and, when he drew his last breath, lost in the boundless cotton-wool sierras of morphine, it was a momentous yet almost beautiful moment.

I had never witnessed finality before. The unsettling stillness, the cancelled eyes that stare up at magnolia. Then someone appoints themselves to brew tea and grill bacon, and it's over.

This may appear callous but, although in many respects he was a good man, he was also an alcoholic prone to occasional violence. We were the recipients, my mother and I, of his internalised rage. Festivites such as Christmas and Easter always marked the onset of weeks of binge drinking. Similarly, we never went on family holidays.

Many of us have imperfect childhoods, and I abhor the confessional booth or the apportioning of blame to others at the diary. But, after years of growing up in an atmosphere of apprehension, the experience does not engender fond reminiscence. To gloss over an inconvenient truth is a form of cheap sentimentality and dishonesty.

I have not spoken with my sister for twenty-five years because of an accident involving a spilt cup of coffee and a white shagpile carpet. It sent her husband into an Olympian sulk, the legacy of which is a profile of pinched, vintage pique. She married young and left home taking her Johnny Mathis records with her. I purged our once-shared bedroom immediately. Later, when Johnny Mathis' homosexuality was revealed in the British tabloid press, she and her husband went into deep mourning. I was ecstatic.

The most enduring, if not fondest, memory I have of my sister is when her husband took her to a West End cinema to see *The Exorcist*. They enjoyed a Chinese meal beforehand. On seeing the scene in the film where the character, Regan, repeatedly stabs at her vagina with a crucifix, my sister slid down in her seat and became violently ill. He escorted her from the auditorium to a London taxi, where she vomited copiously into her cut-price handbag.

On arriving at my parents' home, she was laid out on the sofa next to a hurriedly brought bucket. He placed a cold, damp facecloth on her forehead, as she tried to banish the memory of Linda Blair and the sweet and sour pork at Wong's restaurant. He had to fish the one pound notes from her handbag, carefully removing the contents of her meal under a running tap, before pegging them out on the washing line to dry. Is there a better definition of gallantry? I was behind the living room door, listening to them console each other.

'Oh, love…'

'I know, love.'

'Oh, *love…*'

'Don't, love, *don't.*'

I laughed like a drain.

Regret is futile. It belongs to the realm of the romantic novelist, or to those who lack the stomach for consistency. The family member with whom one has little in common is a bond of bloodline and, sometimes, duty, whereas friendship may be counted upon to hold your ponytail aloft as you vomit into the kerb under the flashing lights of a kebabcotheque. Although, granted, it would take an ardently devoted friend to wash your money after you've "liquidated your assets" into a clutch bag.

As luck would have it, thirty years later a new sister, and a new opportunity arose, by virtue of an affair my father had with a lady from the Isle of Man in 1965. The sole male offspring, I am more of my mother. I take the female line. Helene spent years trying to find me, which is a lavish compliment. She reminds me so much of my father: the bridge of the nose, the countenance, the resilience, the ready laugh. Unfortunately, it was to be a relatively short-lived reunion—we don't speak, either—although this is not due to the accidental kicking over of a black coffee onto a shagpile carpet.

On the Old Kent Road, the two-mile avenue that characterises the successive waves of immigration in the spirit of all great and vibrant cities—Ethiopian phonecard shops, Somalian social centres, Vietnamese takeaways and Bert's Pie & Mash shop still catering to the last of the white working class—the street signage that I once customised is still there. Except that my crayoned "inferno" has been removed and it now directs people to the Mabel Goldwin Community Centre. Which is possibly the same destination.

ROCK AND ROLL SUSANCIDE

AN INQUISITIVE ADOLESCENT LEFT ALONE in the house meddles with the telephone. The internet, of course, did not exist then and some of us were driven purely to alert the world to the actuality of our existence. It was either that or BBC1's *Grandstand*. An exotic steam percolated into the room as the self-appointed Sultana of Sodom spoke.

'Yes?'

'My name is James Maker…'

The artfully arranged pompadour positioned between a half-eaten cold collation and an undusted aspidistra interjected.

'Yes?'

'Well, you see, the thing is…'

'Yes?'

The voice was high Edwardian and summoned up the image of Kaa, the Indian python of Kipling's *Jungle Book*: uncoiling and solicitous, mesmerising you with a mantra before crushing you in its sibilance.

Courtesy of the Infernal Switchboard this was the first important telephone call I was ever to make. I was, in fact, calling the mothership. Feeling isolated and overlooked, I sought the counsel of Quentin Crisp, who was still living in a studio in London's Chelsea with a published telephone number.

I had, in fact, confused the real Quentin Crisp with John Hurt's portrayal of him in *The Naked Civil Servant* which had been broadcast on television the evening before. The latter was a vermilion, lyrical creature addicted to large statements, striding gaily through Bloomsbury while tossing a slipper into the face of ration-book convention. The original version was a study in inertia.

Anti-Hero or Expert Loafer: anyone whose singularity of purpose experiments with a new eye shadow while the night sky rains Luftwaffe bombs is always worthy of attention. Advanced self-absorption requires an effort not only of sustained negligence but also a steel-like composure.

'I'm being ignored.'

I could hear the talons rapidly fanning through the revolving blades of a rolodex of aphorisms and bon mots in search of a suitable card.

Pause.

Tick-tick-*tick*.

'Faint.'

'Faint?'

'FAINT.'

'Thanks, Quentin.'

I followed this advice with diligence, "fainting" whenever it took my fancy; in the queue of the school's canteen, on buses and once in the local public library, until it led to concern for my heart. Not unnaturally, my parents thought I might be epileptic, and on the afternoon of a looming hospital appointment I dug my fingers into the door jamb and confessed:

'I can explain *everything*' – which were also Mussolini's last words.

Two local girls, council estate Lolitas already inescapably doomed, were both involved in seemingly related incidents that amounted to a rash of teenage suicides.

Kneeling on a kitchen work surface and craning my head out of the window, I saw a crowd collect around the star casualties. As Helen Shapiro's 'Keep Away from Other Girls' perkily wafted over the radio they wheeled out Lesley Laycock's toenails, life-lessly poking from beneath a sheet of Irish linen. Swiftly, those toenails glided from view and into the back of an ambulance bound for the borough morgue.

Someone formed the cross, a woman in a headscarf cried with Sicilian relish and Jean, my mother's best friend—and the biggest beehive in Bermondsey—finished off a fish paste bap, folded her arms and announced:

'That Alice Cooper's at the bottom of all this.'

My only thought was: I've just been upstaged.

Jean was the modern Cassandra of our postcode whose predic-tions were often uncannily accurate. She had correctly foretold both the Ugandan uprising of 1974 and the coming of the boiler suit as a utilitarian fashion statement. Sadly, she did not foresee her husband's infidelity with his shorthand secretary and their eventual relocation to a flat above an off licence. Visionaries often see everything, apart from what's happening on their own bingo cards.

She was once overcome by a prophetic vision in the ladies' toilets of the Gaumont bingo hall. She temporarily lost con-sciousness while in the middle of a motion. She was rescued by the assistant manager, who was obliged to climb into the locked cubicle with her. Unceremoniously, she was dragged by the arms through a packed lobby to a waiting taxi.

'Oh, look at the state of her, *shit* all up the back of her tights.'

It was the first and last time that a Scotch egg ever passed her lips on an empty digestive system.

Progressive rock and suicide were all the rage in the mid-1970s. I think one gives rise directly to the other. The entire district broke out in a virus of bumper-sticker optimism and slogan patches pressed to denim. I lived to loathe. When you're a teenager you define yourself by that which you hate, because your personality has yet to accommodate anything except an attention deficit disorder and bedtime resistance. It's the natural progress of puberty and adolescence, but my fledgling seclusion evolved into a self-imposed retreat: Exile on Redlaw Way.

I craved the possibility that the Baader-Meinhof organisation might recruit me, giving me the weapon with which I would assassinate Emerson, Lake *and* Palmer before quickly moving on to Rick Wakeman.

During high school, in a gesture towards assimilation, I invited a school friend to visit me at home. Unbidden, he proceeded to play a Van der Graaf Generator album. I had never heard, until the techno boom of the 1990s, vinyl so crammed with proficient pointlessness. I realise it is a question of taste but I fail to see what progressive rock is for, apart from making life seem to last much longer than it actually is. Even its name is an oxymoron.

I was trapped in a manufactured universe of sonic dross where binary replaces spontaneity; where synthesizer players are the feudal lords of the musical landscape, tackling epic and overarching themes in a macrame choker and a scoop neck smock.

Compared to a forced listening of progressive rock music, the victims of Torquemada's exquisite sadism had it somewhat cushier, I feel. Although the Spanish Inquisition, admittedly, was an exercise in taking masochists *far* beyond their limits.

But prog rock was everywhere and it filled me to the nostrils with semi-sophisticated nihilism. I calmly accepted the whole of Side One while staring at the bedroom door handle in an anguished concentration of telekinesis. When he got up off the bed to play Side Two, I floored him with a desperate rugby tackle, scratched the stylus across the record and asked him to leave.

This he did, and the next day he advertised to the class that I was "unhinged". Unhinged, a curious choice of word for a fourteen-year-old, it made me sound like Flora Robson in *Poison Pen*.

This was one of my better reviews and it worked because people left me alone. I was never bulled at school, which is remarkable considering what I used to turn up in. I wasn't particularly aggrieved at not being popular because, to my mind, almost everybody else was a *cunt* in any case. Besides, I was already formulating other plans.

Suicide. In a distorted idea of romanticism, I believed that if you had not attempted suicide at least once, you were probably not going to be a terribly interesting person when you grew up. Conversely, a pumped stomach of barbiturates identified you as someone whom I'd like to meet. Without entering the dominion of lofty notions, suicide is an unpleasant and serious business but it can also be the ultimate manifestation or protest act; not of frustration and ennui, but of control and even arrogance.

Complex people with a tendency towards self-destruction can be fascinating in a way that someone who is abundant in cheer may never be. In any case, too much cheer in a person is so fatiguing on a practical level alone, because it constantly barrages you with *buoyancy*.

From an artistic standpoint, we know that inner demons and mortal struggle can produce exceptional creativity. Or to rephrase: no one who ever particularly minded whether they were served peas or beans with their oven chips ever galvanised an art movement, or antagonised the public with a small yet vital detail in their daily dress.

I like arrogance in its pure form, which should not be mistook for obnoxiousness. Obnoxiousness is cheap, unbearable and available to anyone. Arrogance can be exciting and infectious; pour charisma into the mélange and you have pure sex. Arrogance misplaced is unattractive, and tends to produce itself in people who are physically too short for the gesture.

I think that the incandescence of self-belief, or at least its appearance, is a necessary ingredient to a certain success. In my case, its form is the execution of the perfect omelette which, in its way, is just as important as Patricia Highsmith.

The evening following the teenage suicide I picked idly at the body of a dead cod and returned to my bedroom.

My sanctum was an amethyst daubed cell decorated with a map of metropolitan New York, which I was determined to use one day, posters of male rock stars dressed in "female apparel", and a sepia newspaper clipping of the Houston mass murderer, Dean Corll. My parents saw it as the building of a shrine to an evident and burgeoning perversity. Obviously, they knew me.

I was forever rearranging what little furniture there was to achieve the effect of a fully self-contained private apartment. There was a balcony that offered an aspect to the surrounding concrete dream of Finnish brutalism, and which remained an unvisited Amazon due to my morbid fear of insects.

After seeing the swish mid-century glamour of *North by Northwest,* I bought a battery-operated telephone. Its wire trailed out under the door and up the stairs to another receiver by the kitchen. My mother could telephone my extension when meals were served. I would collect it on a tray and eat in privacy.

The introduction of this room service arrangement was not precipitated because I felt that I was superior to anybody. It was a civilised form of evasion. Mealtimes were flashpoints that signified parental interrogation over the communal buttering of sliced bread. I cannot take any pleasure in Lancashire Hotpot when I'm being questioned over my toiletry.

'You were in the bathroom for a full hour this afternoon. What were you doing?'

I had been chain-smoking Consulates, feverishly trying to flush them down the lavatory. Only a week lapsed before the telephone vanished with no explanation offered.

Even the witless instinctively knew to reverse gear and avoid a merging miscalculation with a sociopath in training. A few years earlier, the local kids played *Cowboys and Indians* only yards from where I played my own adaptation of what is essentially serialised killing, *Cable Car Crashes*. I would like to have joined them, but even at that tender age I knew that the game was not worth the candle unless there was a bit of rape and pillage involved.

Now what I needed was a full-frontal collision with an express truck loaded with the facts of life.

Am I Einstein or Frankenstein?

I asked myself this same question a decade later in the Raymonde song, 'No One Can Hold a Candle to You'.

One chilly February evening I made my debut as a virgin suicide. I was not about to be upstaged by Mademoiselle Laycock's toenails. I left no note, yet could have said so much. Wrapping myself in a purple, polka dot dressing gown that was, in fact, a silk smoking jacket and arranging my more treasured records around the bed like a collage wreath, I swallowed an entire bottle of Aspirin. Arms crossed, I awaited The End to T Rex through the headphones.

I yearned to be in Manhattan sipping cocktails in the backroom at Max's Kansas City. The party that I wished to gate-crash was in full Mandrax swing—beret knocked at a rakish angle—several time zones to the east while I was uselessly kicking my heels at the Bricklayer's Arms.

Death, you may be surprised to hear, did not come.

During the track, 'Lady', which is far from my favourite song, and quite possibly because of it, I began to feel nauseous. I staggered to the bathroom, opened a bottle of bleach and inhaled deeply to evacuate the pills. It is stressful to survive a suicide attempt least to have to recover secretly. The next morning I awoke with a headache that would have felled a baby hippopotamus.

All that set dressing went to waste. My suicide attempt was *Waiting for Godot* without the car chase sequence. My error was a lack of etiquette. If you're going to commit suicide, issue notice because engagements, pedicures and other people's experiments with pesto can get in the way of your Final Act. Moreover, if you fail to inform them and you survive, they might simply think you have become sloppy in your personal grooming. That may be worse than actual death.

I was alive. A budding putannesca liberally awash with testosterone and lip balm; the arms uselessly and imploringly outstretched; the hair a vaguely coordinated mess of studied chic, I could no longer skirt the question:

'Who will have sex with me?'

An idea popped into my head: speeding motorcyclists. I will throw myself into the path of oncoming motorcyclists. It's not exactly dating, but it's the only option open to me.

The following week, I flung myself in front of a Yamaha RT3 outside the North Peckham Civic Library. I lay in the road, "lapsing in and out of consciousness", until I heard the wail of an ambulance siren. But two things went wrong. The driver was extremely upset, which I had not estimated, and when he took off his helmet, he was clearly over sixty. Realising that my plan had gone awry, I begged the paramedics not to cart me away.

'I don't want any fuss,' I pleaded.

The sexagenarian motorcyclist then proceeded to visit me at home, daily, to assure himself that I was unharmed. Finally, by the fourth visit, I managed to convince him to go away by doing a handstand in the living room. To our mutual relief, he seemed happy with this and stopped coming.

I couldn't even plan a road accident without unwanted complications.

A LEONARD SHORT
OF A TRIO

I WAS NOT A COMPLETE RECLUSE. I did have one friend, a bespectacled girl who lived only five doors away. We were Freaks Reunited. Cherelle. Surprisingly, she was neither black nor French but did harbour a genuine and deep-seated desire to become Jewish at some point.

While other girls were hospitalising themselves in the synchronised hysteria of a gate stampede at David Cassidy concerts, Cherelle did things differently. She instead fell in love with the composer Leonard Bernstein. There then followed an infatuation with the singer and poet Leonard Cohen before transferring her affections back to Mr Bernstein, presumably because the only other Leonard available was Leonard Nimoy of *Star Trek*. She didn't feel quite ready for that.

Her ambition was to be constantly mistaken in a crowded shopping precinct for the American singer, Cher. In this respect, it should be said that her reach was a little shorter than her grasp because she bore an almost unnecessary resemblance to the Greek singer, Nana Mouskouri. I once called her Nana during a childish argument and she sent me a formal letter that stated: "I will never dance in your presence again."

Her mother, certainly, would have felt relieved; Cherelle's

dancing technique was energetic, and she had already contrived to break not one, but two family heirlooms including a vase that had survived the Siege of Mafeking. I replied to her: "I am dismayed at your comportment."

Growing up, we played games of small intrigue. I would recline on her bed wrapped in a large curtain as, head bowed, she knelt and presented herself to me.

'What is your name, child?'

'Esther, Your Highness.'

'I see. Take her away.'

This was rather a short game.

We conceived of another titled *Madame Ennoir* in which a Parisian socialite receives hate mail which, it transpires, is written by the maid who is consequently dispatched back to the mosquito-ridden marshes of the Vendée. I rather enjoyed *Madame Ennoir*, parading around with an eiderdown tied around my waist and sending my playmate out on impossible errands. Cherelle less so, since she nearly always lost the toss of the coin as to who played the disgruntled domestic.

Entering her parents' home was like walking onto the set of a kitchen sink drama from the 1950s. All furnishings and effects appeared to have been purchased immediately after the Second World War. It was a meditation on the many variants of grey, but without the drama of either black or white.

They had a poodle called Lady who barked continually the moment my foot crossed the threshold and who, I suspected, knew that I wasn't to be trusted.

Cherelle called her mother "Ma" and her father "Pa", which

was a strangely American affectation in a Walworth girl. They addressed her as "Girl" to avoid having to shift the vocal stress of her name from the first to the second syllable, as Cherelle correctly insisted.

'I'm not *Che*ryl. I'm Cher*elle*. There's a difference.'

Viewing BBC programming (this was before the advent of colour) they laughed on cue to *Sergeant Bilko* in a tableau that was compellingly Norman Rockwell, save for Cherelle's incongruous habit of wearing little about the house but a pair of knickers. This continued until, at age 15, she was finally ordered to cover herself up. It was quite a relief because Ma, Pa and I seldom knew where to look.

In exchange for running errands, to which my reaction was never less than extreme reluctance, I was given a pocket money allowance. Cherelle and I would gallop over the bridge at St James Road—to our left, Paterson Park, whose swings claimed many a milk tooth—to dine at the Wimpy burger restaurant in the shopping street and market locally called The Blue.

The Wimpy bar is the proto-1950s British burger restaurant chain that offered Brave New World wall murals, plush red vinyl seating booths and served its fare on crockery rather than cardboard.

The waiter would approach the table to take our order. Invariably, Cherelle drank a frothy coffee and ate by proxy as I dined on the 'International Grill'. A platter containing a burger, a frankfurter, bacon, fried egg, chips and a slice of tomato can hardly deserve the appellation, but it sounded special. I once attempted to go à la carte but it caused pricing headaches.

That beloved spot of the pre-teen gastronome, situated in

the northern reaches of a dark and forgotten corner of South London later metamorphosed into a location for modern cinema. It appeared in *Nil by Mouth*, directed by Gary Oldman, where a character is punched in the head immediately on exiting the restaurant. To me, *Nil by Mouth* is really a dramatised documentary.

Also, more recently it appeared in David Cronenberg's *Eastern Promises*, in a scene where Viggo Mortensen, as a Russian Mafia member, negotiates with Naomi Watts for the return of an incriminating diary that documents the misery of an imported Ukrainian prostitute. All exactly where my paper napkin was once placed.

On her fourteenth birthday, Ma and Pa agreed to trim Cherelle's hair by placing a colander on her head and simply chopping off everything around its rim. This can be either groundbreakingly geometric or a total disaster from which one spends months in recovery. It was the latter. Immediately afterwards, she came to my door. Perhaps it wasn't the most tactful of receptions—and, as a Bermondsey cobbler once said to me, 'I can't make shoes out of laces'. I defused the situation with the celebratory cry, 'Mireille Mathieu!'

Gradually, but perceptibly, her mood and demeanour began to change as she became progressively more taciturn and remote. She was always remote, as was I, except for the traffic between our respective bedrooms. I attributed this change to the colander event.

However, a month later she confided to me that she was an insomniac, spending her nights posted at the window spying on a nightwatchman who sat in a little kiosk in the neighbouring goods yard. Mild worry was elevated to high concern when, additionally, she began listening to Helen Reddy's *Angie Baby* on repeat play. This, as we know, is an emergency call.

Soon afterwards, Cherelle slipped a note through my letterbox to tell me that she was being taken temporarily out of school and into hospital to undergo tests. In her accustomed style, she glossed it as a short stay in a Swiss clinic with cable television and 24-hour room service.

As I later understood it, she was diagnosed as suffering with a chemical imbalance in the brain. On asking her parents what, exactly, was wrong with her, I received the alarmingly casual response, 'She's not the full ticket, dear. Flying buttress short of a cathedral. Ha!'

We must remember that, in the 1970s, certain illnesses had yet to be identified or properly diagnosed. Thus, someone suffering from bipolar disorder or acute anxiety, for example, might highly likely have been written off under the generic diagnosis of "GBF": Gone a Bit Funny.

Released from a Lambeth hospital six months later, considerably heavier and wearing impermeably dark purple prescription glasses, she was quite unrecognisable. There was an exotic, somewhat removed, Grace Slick-ness about her, which is quite an achievement at fifteen.

Henceforth, she completed her schooling at home, which in me generated unparalleled envy, and transformed herself into a folk music groupie. She became a fixture at the Cambridge Folk Festival and, somewhat later, in a remarkable act of entrepreneurialism she arranged a concert for the musician, Bert Jansch. It was held at a tabernacle in deepest SE27.

Of course, it isn't simply enough to book a group, one must promote the concert and let people know that the event is happening. Bert Jansch was popular, of that there is no doubt, but his fans did not have the gift of psychic powers. In short, nobody turned up apart from her mother and father, who were very cross indeed. The concert went ahead and, afterwards, her father had to pay the band the sum of five hundred pounds. In 1982, five hundred pounds was not an inconsiderable amount; a family of four could holiday in Tossa de Mar on a half board basis, for less. Thus, a much-anticipated family holiday in Minehead had to be cancelled. The worst of it was that she was completely unrepentant and dismissed it as a "hiccup". Her mother saw this as an undisguised act of cruelty.

I slipped away as she took up with her new best friend: an epileptic, junior book salesman from Islington with a piercing laugh that sounded like a hyena having an unaesthetised Caesarean section. Our paths diverged and we drifted apart. She was drinking Dr Pepper in a peasant skirt and listening to Laura Nyro, which to me was simply gynaecology set to a twelve-string guitar, whilst I was in the nihilistic grip of punk, exploring Piccadilly Circus—which was London's Times Square—and consorting with a cross-dressing rent boy gang called The Elephant & Castle Boot Girls.

Sex and love evaded Cherelle for almost thirty years. Her father died and she continued to tend and care for her mother until, in turn, she passed away only months into the new century.

Cherelle immediately subscribed to a dating agency which paired North American men with English women. After the false promise of a Canadian lumberjack in the Yukon, she met a child psychologist and finally escaped to a new life of synthetic fabrics and air conditioning in New Jersey. Perfect.

I sometimes dream of her even now and wonder what her life must be like. Far, far better I hope. She is untraceable. As transgender people sometimes sever all ties to those whom they formally knew to assert their new identity, Cherelle did likewise.

In the mid-1990s, I recall meeting Cherelle and her mother in the United States. After Pa died, they incessantly crisscrossed North America by train in a sort of paean to Cherelle's earlier obsession with the Beat poets. Montana drifted into Idaho over early morning coffee. Also, I think, as three became two, grief could be deflected provided one kept on the move. Exiting the railroad terminus in Phoenix, Ma—after ten thousand miles of endless prairie—was understandably jaded and wanted nothing more than a sit-down and a decent cup of tea.

We drove to the Grand Canyon which, to my mind, is notable less for its geological splendour than for its effect of instantly silencing children. The transition from seated to vertical standing position negotiated, Ma tottered over to the observation deck. Peering down into the chasm and millennia of tectonic evolution she took a deep breath and exclaimed, in pure Rotherhithe:

'Ooooh, that's a big hole! Where's the cafeteria?'

THE MAX FACTOR
FUNDAMENTALISTS

ON THE 8ᵀᴴ OF DECEMBER, 1980 as the headlines shot
round the planet, sending millions into mourning at his sudden
and shocking demise, I accepted the news of John Lennon's
assassination with calmness because he had the temerity to call
the New York Dolls "a bunch of faggots".

However, to be slain at the steps of one's home is terrible.
Not that I'm suggesting that it's infinitely preferable to be slain
in a local park. But I was never a fan of The Beatles, and neither
can I claim to understand the vast appeal of Paul McCartney.

The New York Dolls are the most important rock group in the
annals of pop history. They symbolised the American underclass
in revolt at a time when cheesecloth ubiquitously occupied every
medium. The New York Dolls precipitated the movement from
smock rock to punk pock. The New York Dolls were tower-
ingly influential. They were way ahead of their time, although
always reliably late at the hairdressers.

My life altered irrevocably the day I returned Lou Reed's *Metal
Machine Music*, an electronic plea for contractual annulment, to
Track & Groove Records on Southwark Park Road for a refund.
Wandering over to a rack stuffed with recorded irrelevance, my

eyes slowly travelled beyond Joni Mitchell's wonderful *Blue*, moved left of Sparks, and promptly froze.

Arrested immediately by an impeccable, monochromatic image of five young men importuning a perfectly innocent couch, vacuum squeezed into leather and stretch vinyl and surrounded by the circumstantial litter of slutdom. I was captive. My life, and my shoe rack, would never be the same.

A more anarchic, cross-dressed car crash of skid row debutantes one could never possibly invent. The front cover of their first album is a masterpiece of pop high art. That sleeve could grace the bedroom door of a 13-year-old in Columbus and tapestry an orchestrated dinner in the Loire.

Beguiling, intimidating and convulsively beautiful, it amplified one message with a swaggering Remy Martin insouciance:

'Well here we are, and if you don't like it, FUCK YOU.'

Many didn't. Everything changed. They shaped my world view forever.

I think there is little argument that, in the winter of 1972, David Johansen called an extraordinary meeting at which he sat everybody down and said:

'From now on, we're all homosexuals, got it?'

To which no doubt Johnny Thunders replied, 'Yes, David, one sees that.'

The New York Dolls debut album is, I feel, a very important document. It was recorded during the period when New York was on the brink of bankruptcy. Intermittent brownouts caused the disenfranchised citizens of Harlem and the South Bronx to go looting and fire-setting; "Dresdenising" their own neighbourhoods and creating an atmosphere that was almost as apocalyptic as Warsaw under the Nazi occupation. This is my New York.

To me, the second most important album is Iggy Pop & The Stooges' vinyl-melting *Raw Power*, especially when cranked up and played through a blown-out Champ amp. The cheaper and lower fidelity the stereo player, the better this record will sound.

I have New York Dolled people to death. But the fact of their influence continues into the 21st century and it cannot be overemphasised. Even today I continue to peep-toe sandal a reference to The Dolls into the briefest of conversations, as if their debut album were released only yesterday. Even small children are not spared. This is the mark of the true zealot.

I know they are not to everybody's taste but I find it unfathomable that anyone can properly resist them. To resist the New York Dolls is to resist the true spirit of rock and roll: pure chaotic energy. *I will never serve in Heaven, but I will fucking reign in Hell.*

They were a four-dimensional, super-animated cartoon strip of a group who, in the sum of their imperfections, achieved perfection.

David Johansen, lead drinker. A collection of curls tossed to one side, a Lucky Strike ever dangling from the lips, a Motormouth Maybelline gravel-drive growl and a countenance indistinguishable from that of a hustler who has just been stiffed for twenty bucks. David Johansen was, transparently, the new Simone Signoret.

Johnny Thunders resembled a switchblade Ronette, his raven hair an enigmatic monument to verticality; his trademark machismo seamlessly offset by an Anna Magnani *weltschmerz*.

Then there was Sylvain Sylvain, a rouged French roller skater escapee from a Marx Brothers movie.

Jerry Nolan looked, and was, as hard as nails; he was poached from a Brooklyn street gang to drum for the troupe.

And Arthur Kane? If you were to sew Dietrich's head onto Frankenstein's body, affix the electrodes, deck the result in a pair of Lurex tights and give it a Schlitz, what you get is Arthur Harold Kane.

As the stylus moved into the run-out groove of 'Jet Boy', I sat there, mouth agape, as if immobilised by a Texas state trooper's stun gun. Seconds passed and, in the ensuing silence, the sheer power of this electric Manhattan missive—its stories strung out like a cheap pearl necklace dipped in Benzedrine—dissolved into my adolescent mind.

Effectively, I had just been coshed over the head, thrown onto the bed and, nitrate jammed into the nostrils, sonically raped. I was irredeemably in love and played their album constantly at a volume that caused my parents to be the recipients of an organised petition.

It was transparent that I had now found a raison d'être: to advertise the prodigious, extravagant actuality of the New York Dolls to the unenlightened by every means at my disposal.

The main thrust of my mission took the form of standing at a busy traffic intersection holding their first album in one hand, while smoking with the other. The lights would turn red at Canal Bridge as a coachload of tourists idly browsed from behind its laminated windows, before returning to the *Frankfurter Allgemeine*. It strikes me now that I was promoting myself as much as campaigning for the New York Dolls but, for me, there was no difference, I *was* a New York Doll.

After a day or two of this, I decided that a more flagrant, self-explanatory approach was needed to ensure a little more attention. Armed with scissors, I cut deep scoops out of the uppers of my platform shoes to simulate women's pumps and wore them barefoot to achieve maximum visibility.

Accessorised by a t-shirt upon which I scrawled NEW YORK DOLLS in red magic marker, I was ready to go to war.

The Old Kent Road was not. After five minutes standing at my usual pitch, cigarette aloft and assuming the composure of someone bored to the depth of his bowels, life started to become interesting. Car horns began blaring and people in moving vehicles screamed abuse. I stood there, murderously trying to look as if I had come from beneath the Gowanus Parkway in South Brooklyn.

More pressingly, two inebriated young men piled out of a nearby pub and began lurching towards me. Payback. Now, I refuse to run because if you're caught the ignominy is doubled, if not tripled. On no account ever say, 'Not the face.' It gives them ideas.

'You look like a fucking *queer*!'

Thank you. At last, someone had got with the programme. They gave me a surprisingly light kicking considering my "crime". It could have been far worse. But that beating signified a catharsis in me. Staunching a bloody nose with the remnants of my crudely daubed t-shirt, I walked home not so much humiliated but instead transformed into a defiant Max Factor fundamentalist. It started something, and once you go down that route, the camino of the exhibitionist, it's very, very difficult to come back.

I was a Doll for life.

1976

NOW EXPOSED AS AN ARCHITECT of tissue-thin deceit,
I squirmed on an antique settle as Dr Friskney began to recite
my letters to Mr Potter.

> *Dear Mr. Potter*
> *Unfortunately, James is unable to attend school for one week because he has*
> *been diagnosed by the doctor as suffering from advanced impetigo of the*
> *lower lip which, as you may be aware, is highly contagious.*
> *Mrs Maker.*

> *Dear Mr. Potter*
> *James' impetigo has now rapidly spread to the upper lip and its immediate*
> *environs. The medicated cream is being applied thrice daily but, at this time,*
> *we feel it inadvisable to allow him to return to school for at least another*
> *week. We are concerned for his nose.*
> *Mrs Maker.*

My mother asked, 'What does "environs" mean?'

Unwisely, I laughed. Three pairs of eyes shot up and drilled
me with stony censure.

It was my parents' second audience with the principal of the grammar school I attended. I despised every brick that built that school and, reciprocally, it hated me. Worse, one had to negotiate two buses and two trains on a disintegrating transport network to reach it.

Dr Friskney was a gowned encumbrance with corns the size of pomegranates who insisted on bringing his bewildered daughter along to open day sports events. She had a lazy eye, so lightning-paced badminton must have been quite a struggle to enjoy.

But it was serious: one more infraction and I would be expelled. Six months previously, I decided to take a two-week sojourn from the women's prison that constituted my education and spent my holiday riding a commuter train up and down a metropolitan branch line.

As the suicide allotments of Selsdon gave way to the semi-detached Betjeman desert of Sutton, I murdered the hours gorging on cheap chocolate, reading Jacqueline Susann's *Valley of the Dolls* and Radclyffe Hall's *The Well of Loneliness*.

'I have nine other letters,' Friskney said, addressing me with a mixture of disapprobation and the sly amusement of someone who knows they have you dangling over the abyss.

'He's quite the novelist. I haven't been able to close my drawer for his handiwork. He'll take double Latin for the next month.'

Double Latin. I'd rather work on the production line of a birdseed factory picking out the husks than memorise the declensions of a dead tongue.

On the first occasion, I was suspended from studies because, with a little help from an adolescent John Galliano, who later bias-cut his way to become a cause célèbre of haute couture, I deliberately fed an Alice Cooper fan's hair into the lathe during metalwork class. This action was provoked by the simple fact that he refused to listen to 'Frankenstein' by the New York Dolls. Also, because his hair was longer than mine.

Consequently, all pupils taking metalwork class were forced to wear an Education Board issued hairnet. Whilst the sight of thirty schoolboys wrestling with this elastic complexity was hilarious, I was Public Enemy Number One until the day I left.

Furthermore, there was the incident when Galliano visited the school chaplain in his office on the second floor to discuss a spiritual matter. I climbed out of the window of an adjacent classroom onto a foot-wide ledge, walking back and forth past the window, and behind the chaplain's head, as if I were an undecided shopper. This attracted an audience in the school car park and I was ordered by the Religious Studies master, who enjoyed taking photographs of the younger schoolboys wrestling with each other on the grassed rugby pitch, to descend.

When Friskney announced this new hairnet safety ordinance from the stage at morning assembly I began to laugh uncontrollably. I was escorted, or rather frogmarched, off the premises by two Christian foot soldiers, one of whom I had successfully seduced, then blackmailed, a year earlier at the school's field study centre in the Brecon Beacons.

It occurs to me that everybody at my school had to, and probably still must, wear a hairnet because of my overtly aggressive New York Dolls fixation. This I consider to be my contribution to the Punk War.

In one sense I was at least spared, in that no one had divined the fact that I would often alight at Forest Hill, ahead of my destination home, to visit my newly acquired boyfriend. Dave was a twenty-six-year-old, self-employed carpet fitter who was eleven years my senior. I met him at the Green Man public house in Great Portland Street, which was the first gay venue I had ever been to.

Naturally, he held a full driving licence. Born to be driven, I am not a motorist and this is my first requisite in anyone who wishes to befriend me. These trysts, which continued for the better part of a year, were strictly illegal on his part and had it come to light he would most certainly have been detained at Her Majesty's pleasure. I love that phrase; it somehow implies that the Queen derives gratification in seeing people banged up.

He once took me to Putney as a carpet fitter's mate, another absence from the school register, but I tripped over an unfurling roll of Axminster, charging headfirst into a treasured glass display cabinet. Miraculously, I was unhurt, although its owner howled with grief, pointlessly trying to reunite two pieces of a twenty-fifth Wedding Anniversary Champagne flute. I was sent to sit in the car and play with the cigarette lighter.

We broke up when I discovered him kissing somebody else in the upper room of The Green Man public house on Great Portland Street. I threw my gin and tonic in his face and walked out, amply protected by the entourage of the Elephant & Castle Boot Girls. He followed suit and tried to run us down in his Vauxhall Viva, mounting the kerb in an attempt to kill me. Passion, we knew how to do that back then.

The summer of 1976 was a long and glorious one. The pavements of South London sizzled with a heat unknown since King George V flatulated on the throne, prompting an outbreak of flying ants that teemed in armies from the cracks between flagstones. Asphalt baked and softened. Every day was a perfect drying day and the washing lines of Peckham were festooned with a Technicolor of flared trousers and lovingly customised waistcoats.

Reggae blasted from jacked up cars, vibrating the kidneys of passing pedestrians; black skin poured into acid yellow hot pants that languished on the bonnet of a Capri; Afros mushrooming ever higher to challenge gravity, each exponent vying to become the Fine Example.

On the steps of unfumigated terraced dwellings that were once villas, girls chain-smoked, endlessly rearranging their hair. Stereo players blared from open windows with the sound of the Sex Pistols—visceral, violent and unrelenting—the pneumatic guitars jamming the ears of unsuspecting listeners with the audio equivalent of erect cock. Cheap, loud recorded noise battling the airwaves with the Aramis scented, happy complacence of its arch enemy.

On the radio, David Bowie's nonsensical, hallucinogenic dance topper 'TVC15' fought for airplay and civilisation with Maureen McGovern's 'The Continental'. I was there at the birth and at the burial of disco.

Saturdays marked the pilgrimage to the King's Road in Chelsea which was, if not the crucible of punk, its Broadway. Semi-dislocated suburban youth flocked here from all points of the compass to shop in its clothes market, to venture into the hallowed temple of Vivienne Westwood's boutique Seditionaries, and to shock the bourgeois ratepayers of Sloane Street with their nonchalance and safety pin nihilism.

I think that the groundswell of punk was more a suburban revolution than an inner city one. Those who lived on the periphery or in the outlying boondocks of a bankrupted, socialist experiment needed rebellion more than anyone else. Punk was a music movement without politics, unless you consider anarchy to be a belief system, and it fizzled out after three years, running dry of sputum.

But punk left us with an important legacy: anyone could form a group. Even me. Attitude is all that counted and you no longer had to figure out a half-diminished guitar chord to be a musician.

One cannot guess what the musical landscape would look like today had the punk revolution never happened. Certainly, rap, which to my mind is the counterpart of punk on the family tree, might never have been invented.

A modern metaphor for punk is the Swedish *conquista* of the 1980s, when the Vikings came back to divest us of our chintz and convert our sensibilities back to simplicity and functionalism.

I wandered the King's Road in my plastic sandals, Oxford bags and Ramones t-shirt with Tony. Tony was an Anglo-Turkish Cypriot kid who shared my enthusiasm for David Bowie and T Rex and whom I met through a friend from primary school. The Anglicisation of his name from Tahir suited him because he looked a little like a very young Tony Curtis.

He was slightly shorter than me, a little more flesh, naturally cheerful and with a keen sense of humour. He lived close by on Ilderton Road with his fearsome mother. As with Lady, Cherelle's poodle, she too knew that I was not to be trusted.

We became good friends and would travel together to hang

out at a leather shop he introduced me to that was frequented by punks, gays and fetishists in the King's Road market. The proprietors were a couple of forty-something leather queens who were known as Mr and Mrs Fenner.

Mr Fenner was masculine in the gay San Franciscan style of the 1970s: moustache and short preppy hair but emerging from behind the counter to reveal leather chaps worn over his Levis. Mrs Fenner was a pigskin Pollyanna.

For some, life really is lived as one long protracted comedy sketch which they, and us, are unable to escape from. Overweight and perpetually out of breath, Mrs Fenner martyred himself to deep vein thrombosis. The personality had long since been surrendered to the purpose of public entertainment. Every sentence uttered began and ended with a bold exclamation mark, which is enormously tiring, especially for the listener.

Nevertheless, he was the matriarch and counsellor to the assortment of Mohican waifs and strays who bought nothing but colourfully draped themselves over the merchandise as living decoration.

Leaning across the counter in mock confidentiality his first words to me were, 'Why is my punishment so *endless*?!'

It was a question that forebade answer as, clearly, he adored every excruciating minute of it. I felt as if wedged in the front row of the circus of fear, hypnotised by a glove-puppet cobra whose eyes could not be accommodated by their sockets.

'Thrombosis at my age! I'm only 35! You'll never know the agony!'

He broke off to speak to an invisible, itinerant Belgian seamstress called Yvette who deftly stitched away behind a heavy felt curtain that shielded her from questioning by the Home Office.

Someone had turned up the volume on the record player as The Village People's 'San Francisco' blasted out from the speakers, and he was now shouting.

'Don't say anything to Mr Fenner, but I don't know how long I can carry *on* like this!'

I don't know what happened to Mr and Mrs Fenner. What I do know is that the market no longer exists. The punks drifted away before receding altogether, retreating to whence they came to become a new generation of parents. Those who continued to fight the battle either eventually overdosed, lost their hair to amyl nitrate addiction or forged expense account careers in a media that rapidly globalised the world, overdosing the rest of us on *them.*

Autumn arrived with unpredictable and spectacular thunderstorms. The plastic sandals that had once assured passage across three London boroughs suddenly fell apart, on cue. Michaelmas re-entered the calendar and Disco Mysticism arrived with the holy terror of Abba's unstoppable 'Dancing Queen'. 'Dancing Queen' is not merely a song; it is a tyranny and a reliable instrument of torture.

"You are the dancing queen, young and sweet, only forty-six…dee-dum dee-dum dee-dum."

This was my last year at school.

ELEPHANT AND CASTLE BOOT GIRLS

'IF YOU DON'T PUT THAT LIPSTICK ON we're gonna tear out your riah and kick the fucking living daylights out of you. Have you got that, doll?'

* "riah" is Polari for hair. Polari is a mixture of slang and Mediterranean Lingua Franca popularised by British gay men.

It was 1977, the year of the Queen's Silver Jubilee. Another queen, Maude, menacingly challenged me with an opened tube of Revlon lipstick. Tall, hook-nosed and with non-retractable claws, Maude resembled a stretched version of the child catcher in *Chitty Chitty Bang Bang*. The others circled me. Martha, Jesse and Fred. I glanced at Tony who was an honorary member of the Elephant and Castle Boot Girls and who had introduced me to them.

The Elephant and Castle Boot Girls used to gather outside the ticket hall of the Elephant and Castle tube station before riding the train to the West End to visit either The Green Man public house or Spatz nightclub on Oxford Street.

Bedecked in au courant male fashion accessorised by female attire—a silk scarf, sandals and a weapon of choice, usually a small vegetable knife—they would smoke ostentatiously while despatching the Northern Line passengers who passed beneath their collective, stylistic sneer. Some, returning from the subterranean depths, eyes still blinking, to be impaled by a maliciously observed detail. Women, particularly, were deconstructed on the spot.

'*Not* blue eye-shadow with that coat, love.'

You messed with this lot at your peril. They were hardened rent boys who may have been effeminate but exhibited a pathology that bordered on the savage. How else could one survive in such circumstances or, indeed, in that locale looking as they did?

This was the Old Kent Road: home of boxing clubs, the Millwall FC Bushwackers and a sprinkling of pubs where, if your testosterone level was anywhere below critical mass, you could expect to weekend in Guy's Hospital.

One of the public houses along that delightful avenue, which established Belfast-style blackout windows well before they became fashionable, was The Dun Cow. Never has a venue been so aptly named for that is exactly the condition in which many a soul staggered through its doors with dislodged teeth: *a done cow*.

Ironically, The Dun Cow is now a dental surgery. It stood opposite the Thomas A'Beckett which was famous for its boxing ring above the saloon bar where the heavyweight champion Sir Henry Cooper once trained. The boxing room has been removed and it is now a gastropub. Whether they trust their clientele with steel cutlery is not something I can answer.

I took the lipstick from Maude's proffered claw, whereupon Martha stuck a compact mirror in my face. I didn't want to be in a gang, especially this one, but I had now run into them and avoidance would have meant hugely altered travel plans. As Fred encouraged me, I applied the lipstick to my lips generously, for it hardly mattered now.

'Don't worry, we'll be here when you come back.'

'Come back?'

'Yes,' said Maude, stepping forward. 'Just do one round of the block, up to the Walworth Road and then back down The Elephant.'

'And don't run,' added Martha.

500 yards—or if you're metric, a half-kilometre—through enemy territory in Revlon's Sudden Change. Given my exploits a couple of years earlier, a little further up the road with my New York Dolls album sleeve, it didn't quite daunt me as much as it might anyone else. I was given a send-off of cat-calls and strode up to the Walworth Road with my best "approach-me-not" expression. Scowling, in other words.

On turning into the busy bus traffic of the Walworth Road, I immediately saw a group of black teenagers coming in the other direction. This was a truly South London "Oh My Gawd" moment. The only options available were either retreat, which was unthinkable, or a prize bingo arcade. Momentarily, I sought refuge next to a woman whose felt-tip pens expired one after the other as the caller announced numbers at an impossible rate.

'These fucking *pens*!'

When the coast was clear, I made progress towards Elephant Road which is a quiet side street lined by railway arches. Nothing is likely to occur here, I thought. Wrong. Two men in work overalls were taking a break from painting the door of one of the storage lock-ups. One of them was halfway through a sandwich when he saw me sauntering past, eyes glued ahead of me.

"Ello darlin'!'

Here we go.

"E's wearing lipstick! Oi mate!'

"Oi mate" is not a greeting but a prelude to violence. I broke into a canter until I reached the corner and, decreasing my pace, returned to the light applause of my reception committee.

'You're alright by us,' Fred nodded approvingly.

'Come and have a Wimpy,' said Maude.

'Do you like my hair like this?' Martha asked, scrunching a stray curl.

'Yes, it's an improvement,' I answered.

Martha looked at me levelly.

'Maude?'

'Yes, Martha?'

'Stick another pin in that doll?'

Everybody laughed good-naturedly and off we went into the shopping centre.

I knew them for only a few months. Maude, Martha and Jesse lived together on the thirteenth floor of a tower block on Newington Butts which they shared with a middle-aged Jamaican woman whose function was that of unofficial maid. How this domestic arrangement came about I'm unsure, but she was evidently in need of psychiatric care.

The Elephant and Castle Boot Girls introduced me to the lights and the underground drinking dens of the West End. It was the world of hustlers and punters, frowsy hostesses and night people. Also, purple hearts, Nembutal, Dexedrine and hard liquor. It was a revelation to these fifteen-year-old eyes.

They took me to a party in East London where I drank strong Pilsner lager and took amphetamine for the first time. Subsequently I vomited all over the record turntable and Candi Staton's 'Young Hearts Run Free'. This was extremely bad form that marked me as a novice. They stripped me and threw my clothes into a bath of cold water. When eventually I awoke, lying next to a couple in full sexual congress, I could only think of how to get home.

I walked from Bromley-by-Bow to Bermondsey via the Rotherhithe Tunnel dressed only in shoes and a belted raincoat. Underneath I was naked, carrying my soaking wet clothes in the crook of my arm.

On arrival at Redlaw Way, my father greeted me in the hallway with a look of disgust and unspent rage. He opened his mouth, clearly about to cannonball me with the speech he had been rehearsing until the early hours. I put up my hand, the palm facing him and slurred, *'Don't.'*

Swaying into my bedroom to a tirade of recriminations, I collapsed onto the bed, rolled off and broke a Depression-era standard lamp. We didn't speak for a fortnight.

Weeks later, Tony and I met at the tube station intending to go to The Green Man. He had scarcely arrived, in a suit reminiscent of Bette Davis in *A Stolen Life*, when, on his heels, appeared the Turkish Mafia. They were three in number. His mother, whose fierce comportment readily explains the success of the Ottoman Empire; his visiting chemistry student cousin from Ankara and the feared Uncle Shenel who, in the absence of a father, had become Tony's guardian.

We were both escorted back to the house on Ilderton Road, forbidden to neither speak nor offer explanation, and marched into the living room. Tony was at the point of blubbing under the vigilant, fanatical gaze of Uncle Shenel. Tea was served in deafening silence before the Inquisition began.

Narrowing her eyes, his mother looked at me in a way that suggested there were thumbnail screws in the onyx cigarette box placed between us.

'Why you try to be like woman?'

'I'm not trying to be a woman,' I snapped.

'We go to see your mother. Where she live?'

The eyes were now slits.

'Oh, that's impossible. She's had a stroke.'

'What is stroke?'

Tony translated.

'Oh darling, that is terrible. Then you must go to her.'

I darted for the door.

I didn't see Tony for almost six months. He was grounded and kept housebound under threat of Uncle Shenel setting fire to his mattress, with him on it. Subject to a Turkish restraining order, I was not allowed to visit him anymore. I was a corrupting, Western influence.

News reached me that he had run out of moisturiser. No friend may stand by in such a grave situation. So, as he dangled a rope out of an upstairs window, I filled the small wicker basket attached to it, and he hastily drew it up. That's friendship. I do not define friendship by unconditional loyalty; that is for pets, not people. Friendship is the selfless act of providing others with a necessary restorative in a time of need.

Uniquely, I decided to concentrate on my upcoming examinations in readiness to go out into the world. To do what, I had no idea.

MORRISSEY

MY NEW FRIEND. WHOM I'D MET only four hours ago, was considerably more fleet of foot in his white gym plimsolls than me. They were the last thing I saw as he accelerated with the commendable alacrity of Zola Budd and shot past me into the distance, before those uncouth hands wrenched at my jacket.

One sees this in wildlife programmes: the slavering pack of hyenas that gang up on the proud, beautiful mother cheetah to bring her down. But this cheetah was wearing cork heel boots, which tends to slow you up on the Serengeti of Central Manchester.

In September 1977, the *New Musical Express* had published another of his letters exhorting them to give more press coverage to the bands of the post-glam New York scene. I had seen his name a few times and felt compelled to contact him as he was the only other living New York Dolls fan viewable through my opera glasses.

They had printed his full address, which I submitted to Directory Enquiries who gave me his home telephone number, not realising what they were doing. Courtesy of the Infernal Switchboard, this was the second most important call I was to make.

'Operator, can you put me through to Manchester 666-7125?'
Momentary silence.
The click of buttons.
Connection.
Two hundred miles distant the calm of a damp, Stretford hallway was violently broken by the electronic trill of a 1970s Trimphone.
'Yes?'
The young man's voice was soft and hesitant.
'Steven Morrissey?'
A kettle began to scream in the background.
'Yes?' Mildly distracted.
'Hello. My name is James Maker. I am savagely distorted but I'd like to discuss the New York Dolls.'

The soon-to-be one of the most important lyricists of the century met me at the ticket barrier of Piccadilly station earlier that afternoon. I immediately saw that he had been putting on a brave front since 1959, resisting both decimalisation and new fabrics. He immediately saw...a bowler hat.

He looked like Patti Smith dressed as Dee Dee Ramone and carried a satchel stuffed with vitamin pills and blank postcards. He would liberally distribute these postcards, upon which he scrawled cryptic messages, at bus stops, telephone booths and pubs.

One might sit down in the snug of a bar to sip a milk stout, or an amontillado if you were feeling continental, only to find a card pinned under the ashtray bearing the communiqué: I ENJOY EMPHASIS IN THE WRONG PLACE.

Alternatively, perusing a bus schedule, ice-cream in hand,

en route into town to buy that pair of new fashion jeans, one finds a postcard slipped under the fibreglass mounting. Curious, you tease it out: YAWNING EMPTINESS DEMANDS EVER MORE DIMINISHING TREATS.

The emergency door at the back of the bus flew open and three pairs of impressively large but badly manicured hands reached in and tried to drag me out. They had tasted blood and they wanted more. I'd already been kicked to the ground for wearing a bowler hat on a Saturday afternoon in the middle of Manchester's Piccadilly Gardens but, luckily, a sexagenarian couple intervened before my cranium was booted in.

'I want you off this bus,' the driver shouted.

We had fled to a waiting bus after the kicking incident. We huddled behind two people and their dogs to form part of a queue, hopelessly trying to blend in, when we realised that they were blind and had no idea what was going on. There was no one that we could appeal to. We were spotted again and, as the gang drew near, we ran onto this bus, bound for Lower Broughton.

Outside, seven pairs of tattooed fists graphically expressed their desire to drive their chunky sovereign rings into our pretty little faces. I had escaped the grabbing hands only by accurate and vicious deployment of my cork heel boots and we had moved to the front, away from the emergency door, sitting there rigid with obstinacy.

Morrissey has been compared to many people, notably Oscar Wilde, but on that afternoon he was the Rosa Parks of Old Trafford. We knew that to leave this vehicle meant hospitalisation for him, and a slow execution for me. Honestly, all this fuss over a bowler hat.

'Well this wouldn't have happened in London,' I said sniffily, as if someone had served me a plate of cucumber sandwiches without the crusts cut off.

'I refuse to give up my seat on this bus,' said Morrissey, quietly but firmly.

'You are refusing to leave this bus?' replied the driver, nostrils flared, godawful kipper tie.

'Yes. I refuse to alight.'

The arms were folded. Unbudgeable.

A Morrisseyean tactic. Some people advance by fighting and struggling and pushing and scratching; others advance by simply not moving at all. In effect, the locomotion is driven by the force of inertia. Checkmate.

The other passengers grew restless, complaining to the back of my bowler hat. The driver eventually relented, slamming the bus into gear as we all lurched out of the bus station into horizontal, Manchester rain. The beer monsters ran alongside us and, in a misguided act of appeasement, I threw coins at them out of the air vent of a side window.

'You shouldn't have done that,' said my friend, staring studiously ahead while, inches away, a face utterly contorted with unspent hatred bellowed heavily-brewed obscenities in a Crumpsall accent at the pane of glass separating us.

'But what do they want?' I asked, beginning to feel bruised as the adrenaline subsided.

'You', he said, matter-of-factly, popping a peppermint into his mouth.

Arriving back at Maison Morrissey I was introduced to his mother, Elizabeth Dwyer, a slim and attractive lady who worked as a librarian. It was not the smoothest of meetings because, perhaps still nervous from our unexpected casting in a wildlife documentary, I inexplicably asked, 'Are you Scottish?'

We climbed the stairs to his bedroom with a pot of tea and played the whole of *Horses* by the Patti Smith Group.

The young Morrissey garret was a microcosm of pop symbolism. The walls were covered in large, framed photographs of the New York Dolls and James Dean along with a signed print of the British comedy actress Esma Cannon. A Remington typewriter was positioned under a window that looked out to a small and scarcely-used garden where the family cat, Tibby, was buried. Mournfully, not buried deep enough as Tibby had a propensity to resurface in heavy rainfall.

There was a bookcase stuffed with classic English literature, modern American titles, film compendiums and feminist writing. All along the floor of one wall were stacked a raft of vinyl records in alphabetical order. It was an enclosed world, seemingly independent of its surroundings, which could have been either a sanctuary or a cell depending upon one's taste in curtains.

But, certainly, it was from within these four walls that were formulated many of the ideas and themes one would later see in their various manifestations: words, sleeve designs, videos.

It was midnight. I expect that I had not eaten since before boarding the train in London earlier that morning. I asked him whether I could have some cheese before retiring to bed.

'You should by rights be on a mortuary slab at this stage, and your primary concern is cheese?'

Thus began a friendship and a correspondence spanning more than three decades. One could identify his missives—even though the Penny Black might have fallen off—by the now famous Morrissey font and the whiff of household damp on manila.

Occasionally, he took the train to London for the weekend. The unvarying feature of these visits was that one could always rely upon incident. On March 10, 1980, we witnessed what we believed to be a flotilla of alien spacecraft silently gliding across the night sky of Rotherhithe, heading towards the northwest. Willesden, probably. Instinctively, I telephoned a UFO Research Centre to report the sighting and packed a small tartan bag with my favourite singles and a change of underwear in case we were invaded.

Later, he asserted that it was an optical illusion occasioned by the Aurora Borealis bouncing off the lens of my National Health prescription spectacles, but some people are in denial of alien visitation.

It was clear from the outset that we were both patients, in adjacent beds, whose tenure on the Ambrosine Phillpotts ward was indefinite.

Where friends might ordinarily enjoy embarking on outings together, perhaps the cinema, a club, a gallery or a trip to the seaside, our friendship was principally grounded in shared, somewhat indoor activities.

Although, we did once risk Blackpool, commandeering a Mini Cooper and an acquaintance as chauffeur; Morrissey remaining steadfastly at ground level as I whooshed past him, then above him before hurtling *towards* him, waving from a variety of fairground rides in a fit of ubiquity.

Those indoor activities are, metaphorically speaking, perhaps best understood as the over-rehearsal of a very long, existentialist play titled *Death* in a small hall courtesy of a Liberal council, but without ever actually putting it on.

Indeed, in the gabardine Manchester of the late 1970s and early 1980s, living under a sky so perpetually opaque that you questioned whether you were living inside a Tupperware container, extinction had been seen off on so many fronts. Poverty, creeping mold and continual letterbox rejection: the idea of death was no longer a matter of dread but one of plain, biscuit-crumbed curiosity.

He may always rely on me to telegraph the news of a film star's demise: 'Deborah Kerr. Dead. 2.30AM Pacific Standard Time. A bit bland, I thought.' And I can rely on him to consistently slide the abacus against my true age. It is an arrangement that one understands.

There has been some considerable, blunt-pencilled twaddle and highly deduced inaccuracies written about Morrissey in the attempt to pierce the persona, expunge the myth and divine the man's inner life.

We love to solve mysteries because they are irresistible. But, in tearing away at the mortal bandages to demystify why someone has touched you, there is the critical risk that one destroys the attraction that led you to them in the first place. It's rather like loudly itemising the reasons why you find your partner's lovemaking so pleasurable, *during* the act.

In my opinion, there has been published only one incisive

biography on Morrissey and its title is *Saint Morrissey*, written by Mark Simpson. One book, which I will not name because I don't want to give its author any publicity, is a fictional chronicle of poor construction that places me sliding down a banister in a theatrical pub in Huddersfield in 1978. I have never visited Huddersfield, neither as a day tripper, a pop singer or a door-to-door agent for Avon. Though, naturally, I am acquainted with the "Banister Technique".

Johnny Rogan's exhaustive, gumshoe detective story *The Severed Appliance*—for in 1987 when The Smiths ended, Morrissey felt as if disconnected from a kidney dialysis machine—interviewed everyone from the survivors of the Irish Diaspora to a girl sat on a wall at the local Arndale Centre eating a packet of crisps. It is unique in that by the time you have reached the conclusion of this tome, you know less about them than when you spyglassed its comprehensive acknowledgements page.

Of course, since the highly-anticipated publication of Morrissey's own 'Autobiography', the aforementioned are even less alluring.

Morrissey refused to give up his seat on life's bus. There had been an interlude as singer with The Nosebleeds and an association with guitarist Billy Duffy (later of The Cult) whom I knew briefly in London, but the project was short-lived despite having received a glowing concert review in the *New Musical Express*.

He became good friends with Simon Topping, the lead singer of the Flixton-based group A Certain Ratio, carrying out managerial duties including the collection of ticket payments at their earlier concerts. They were initially born of the post-punk movement but later evolved into a dance/funk fusion that would later influence The Happy Mondays.

Another local group who captured the eyes and ears of a young Steven Patrick was The Stockholm Monsters. Morrissey invited them to support The Smiths at Glasgow Barrowlands. For no apparent motive, their singer pasted the stage with wads of chewing gum, necessitating a restricted physical performance on the part of the headlining act's chanteuse.

Life returned to its familiar pattern of moving an overburdened toaster with a faulty spring from one melamine surface to another. Of interminable matinees stationed by the bay window of the living room. And of continually being ignored by the Factory Records impresario Anthony Wilson, who ingeniously discovered and promoted every talent in Manchester except its interresting.

Then, in 1982, hope one day arrived in the form of a skinny boy from Ardwick who could play the guitar. The rest is over-documented history.

I feel that Morrissey has achieved the impossible. It is the straightforward that eludes him. He had to become famous because, although he is a savant in the auditorium, he is a dead loss in a launderette.

I left London to migrate to Manchester because, at that time, it was the most interesting place to be in the world if you had a personality disorder and a good record collection. Although leaden, oppressively Victorian and in the grip of a severe economic downturn it was, in modern parlance, full of crushingly hip people.

Ugliness and strife is often the niece of creativity; which is why a superb view of Lake Geneva and a cordon bleu menu has perhaps never inspired an original couplet.

In 1980 I met his longstanding friend, Linder. I arrived at a house on Mayfield Road in Whalley Range where Morrissey, Linder and an assortment of other tenants shared rooms. I had not told him of my impending arrival.

He returned from the communal bathroom to find a skinhead (my new look) with no immediate plans, sitting on his bed, smoking and playing *Things Your Mother Never Taught You* by Wayne County and The Electric Chairs.

At once, he suggested that I audition as bass player for Linder's group, Ludus. Transparently, this was a ruse to get rid of me at the earliest opportunity because I have never demonstrated the slightest aptitude for the stringed instrument.

'I can't play bass,' I protested.

'They're an improvisational jazz band. Nobody will notice.'

Ludus' avant-garde, tampon-draped experimental jazz oddity was not really my worldview but I saw it as significant and provocative at a time when the Women's Movement, as it was then termed, was only beginning to gather pace. It was an audition remarkable only for its brevity, and it was a slender escape for the both of us.

Morrissey and Linder regularly wandered the vast Southern Cemetery of Manchester, which is a gothic Manhattan of the departed. In those days, many pastimes were free and did not require expensive peripherals. They enjoyed reading the gravestones of millworkers and clog makers who once lived in the gaslight of the Industrial-era.

On noting the neglect of the long-forgotten graveside of "MILDRED STENCH. 1866 – 1886. SPINSTER", Morrissey was determined to form a group called Graves of Spinsters. The Smiths were almost going to be Graves of Spinsters. In fact, one of them was.

However, it was there that they saw a tatty old van parked at the gates with "Sex Pistols" sprayed on the side of it together with a small flyer advertising, "Tonight at the Lesser Free Trade Hall".

Linder entered my life again, albeit invisibly and momentarily, when in 2004 she cancelled her appearance at the Move Festival at Old Trafford on a bill featuring Morrissey, the New York Dolls and myself. In short, she disagreed with the running order and believed that she was entitled to be billed above me. It was unfortunate because Linder is a very interesting artist and I would like to have met with her again.

The unpalatable truth is that someone who has not released a record since Margaret Thatcher closed the whole of Nottinghamshire—because she felt like it—is not entitled to take the stage after someone who is modestly unpopular but with an actual single in the charts.

October 4th, 1982.

'Mesdames et messieurs. Ce soir j'ai l'honneur de vous introduire The Smiths. Je suis sûr qu'ils vont fair BOUM ici et je suis certain que leur musique vous fascinera.'

The intro music of Klaus Nomi's 'The Cold Song' evaporated into the ether as I took to the stage at the Ritz Club to announce The Smiths' debut concert in a blue mohair suit and court shoes. Whereupon Johnny Marr plinked into 'Reel Around the Fountain' or 'Reel Around Joan Fontaine' as it was affectionately coined.

I was never "The Fifth Smith". There was never a strong desire on my part to become a member of The Smiths. I am far too Susan Hayward to share the spotlight with anybody else. Morrissey invited me to appear with The Smiths as a guest. I was to present them in French, to dance in a cool and understated manner—within the chalked circle he had drawn for me—and to sing backing vocals on 'What Do You See In Her?' I was also given a pair of maracas.

The high heels component was not borne of camp or frivolity but of an intellectual devotion that originates in the revolutionary, sexual ambiguity of The New York Dolls. I also wore them because I felt like it.

I appeared at two concerts, The Ritz and The Manhattan, both in Manchester. It was over before you could fire Dale Hibbert. I cannot recall Mr Hibbert, although I believe he played bass at the debut concert. I fancy he has one of those faces one could live with for twenty years yet instantly misplace. Forthwith, and after The Manhattan, The Smiths were a four-piece group.

Their manager at the time, Joe Moss, a wholesale clothing retailer, expressed grave reservations at my live participation. He was very keen to push me through that very same ticket barrier at Manchester's Piccadilly railway station, and to see me off, because he felt that I was a distracting influence. Well, he was right.

Johnny Marr was slight, intense, stylish and appeared friendly.

Mike Joyce and Andy Rourke were affable yet tended to circle rather than approach me directly. Initially, Joyce and Rourke were not particularly comfortable with the connotations of Morrissey's prescient homoeroticism, and my presence was deemed further proof of this.

The title of 'What Do You See In Her?' was changed to 'Wonderful Woman' for this very reason because of a concern by Joe Moss that the group might be construed as gay. His tenure as their manager was brief.

It was evident from the beginning that the songwriting, the conceptualisation of the group's identity and the public voice of The Smiths lay exclusively in the hands of Morrissey and Marr. Consultation with Rourke and Joyce was superfluous in this respect. Morrissey, for example, did not telephone Andy Rourke to discuss pantone colours for the sleeve art.

I believe Joyce made a laddish *faux pas* at an early, yet important interview. It was his first and last cough into the microphone at a press conference. One might say that the vision of The Smiths was almost Thatcherite in its unyielding and uncompromising mission.

The partnership of Morrissey and Marr is comparable to that of John Lennon and Paul McCartney and, later, Elizabeth Taylor and Richard Burton, in that it was a marriage of almost licentious fecundity. So prolific were they, and in such abundance did they produce rather perfect vinyl gems at a time when many worshipped at the temple of Hazell Dean, that potential hit singles were routinely consigned to B-side status. They could afford to be spendthrift.

One intoxicating cyclone presaged another, each one exhilaratingly shorter than its predecessor until, with 'William, It Was Really Nothing', we are at less than two minutes — if you discount the backwards guitar outro. This is what pop music should be.

By 1984 they were an inevitability and Morrissey's face loomed from every magazine cover from *Record Mirror* to *Cheshire Life*. In fact, one couldn't look up at the television in the dental surgery—latex hands tampering with eye-wateringly expensive bridgework—without witnessing 'Heaven Knows I'm Miserable Now' peaking at Number 10 in the Hit Parade.

The truth is, we do hate it when our friends become successful, because it sharpens the aperture of our own circumstances. Everything changes. You are stirring a pot of baked beans, cocking an ear to the local evening news, while they assess a penthouse in an upcoming city break destination. You would have to be a person who has never known ambition not to feel envious. But, you can respond to this in either a positive or a negative way.

It was at Morrissey's Cadogan Square apartments in London's Chelsea, within paces of where Oscar Wilde once lived, that I met Sandie Shaw when she was enjoying a return to the stage and television performing Morrissey and Marr compositions.

I have always thought of Sandie Shaw as the Nico of Dagenham and, to this day, I still feel a pleasurable shiver at 'Long Walk Home', released in 1966. With the mild success of 'Hand in Glove' and 'Please Help the Cause Against Loneliness' she was naturally keen to consolidate her comeback. So keen, in fact, that she contrived to enter his apartment building, without a key, and proceeded to ring the doorbell.

She is an Essex girl and there is nothing like the direct

approach. But with Morrissey, the direct approach or the approach without charm, rarely works. One must learn to play canasta. We were in the sitting room listening to the musical score of her doorbell chiming when we decided to move across the hallway to the adjacent kitchen for some much-needed refreshment.

Adopting the Leopard Crawl, a military manoeuvre designed to advance oneself with the smallest silhouette possible, the body close to the ground, we chanced our luck and stealthily crept towards the kettle. Halfway across the hallway, the letterbox flapped open.

'I can see you. Open up.'

He wasn't the only one to have a woman shout through his letterbox that year. I threw a twenty-fifth birthday party, or soirée, at my flat. A soirée is a party where the invited guests should number not less than seven and no more than fourteen. I had invited my old friend Lyndsay, but she arrived with three gate-crashers and there followed a dispute through said letterbox.

'Let us in.'

'I can let *you* in, but not *them*.'

'Why?'

'Because I'll be over my limit and it won't be a *soirée* anymore.'

Fast forward thirty years: I was in brief email correspondence with Sandie Shaw when I recorded 'Long Walk Home', which she released as the B-side to the single 'Run'. She liked my version and said that she, too, would like to re-record it. Instinct told me not to encourage her, and as an extra precaution I hung a heavy curtain over my front door, and letterbox.

You don't have to like 'Alsatian Sister' to acknowledge that Morrissey is a true icon in the authentic and classic sense. Captivating the hearts of outsiders of all colour, creed and sideburn arrangements, he possesses an interior androgyny that, through songs of truth—or his truth—immaculately condensed, provides a catalyst for the expression of emotions in an audience that otherwise might not be able to articulate them.

Therefore, Morrissey's appeal is as popular with hod carriers, Mexican gangbangers and university graduates as it is to mature transvestites on legal aid. Within the grooves of his arsenal is a harmony of noise, voice and incidental suicidalism that has not been heard since David Bowie circa 1972. Yet he is never depressing. Melancholy is spiked with the paprika of wit and drenched in Kalahari-dry humour. He is a "miserablist" only in the sense that one cannot moonwalk to his songs.

On a purely literary level, Morrissey's lyricism makes him a more interesting artist than many celebrated writers. This is not overblown lip service, it is pop fact.

Morrissey, along with David Bowie, implicitly grasps and understands the mechanics of image and the power that it can harness. He is a master of dualism, whether in language or in the expertly distressed retrosexual jeans offset by the depiction of an Algonquin Round Table eminence on a t-shirt.

The terraced Salford soliloquy is sometimes landscaped by a widescreen Bogdanovich vision of Midwestern America. The pulp fiction novella titles masquerade lyrics of uneasy depth and songs of myriad sexual perspectives.

It is this dualism that makes him such an enigmatic, intriguing and unquantifiable nut to crack. The Californian highway signpost leads not necessarily to Zuma Beach, but to an Eccles cul-de-sac. It is the navigation of absurdism and genius.

He has outlived at least two dozen people who once worked with him. The Last of the International Playboys is, to me, more symbolic of The Last of the Theatrical Professionals, by which I mean professionals who work in theatre, not professional theatrics, although we have all had our moments. I see the roll call as this:

Joan Crawford.

Gladys Cooper.

Joan Littlewood.

Gladys Henson.

Morrissey.

In the expanse of time that I have known him, there has never been a partner or long-term girlfriend, or boyfriend. Exactly why this should be so is an enduring conundrum.

However, it is true that the longer one lives alone the more one becomes accustomed to, if not steeped in, one's own marmalade. As one passes into maturity, domestic routine becomes an ineluctable destiny. One might yearn for companionship, but not at the cost of someone marching in and altering a perfectly good kitchen roster that has suited you since Bananarama disbanded.

Morrissey is an underrated, good plain cook. A ratepayer and a pragmatic householder who enjoys simple pleasures. While the restaurants of Lausanne or Rodeo Drive overflow with Chanel and high laughter, he is more at home with a selection of speciality breads and a viewing of Donald Pleasence in *The Caretaker*. Three hundred times. His spiritual home is neither Los Angeles nor Stretford but, in fact, Sidcup.

Unimpressed by stellar fame, he does not deal in the currency of showbiz. This is the "Stretford Factor" of having lived the first twenty years of life stretching a ten pound note into a fortnight's provisions while being at the mercy of GM Buses' experimental livery.

There is something of the unrealised sportsman about him in his nimbleness at outwitting unwelcome pursuit, as once occurred with Erasure at Heathrow Airport by the tactical use of both up and down escalators to thwart their Lycra.

Erasure were to momentarily pop into my life when RPLA were recording at Air Studios. The studio door swung open and someone in a neoprene leotard cheerily trilled, 'Hiyas!'

I turned in a revolving chair, dragged on a Dunhill and replied: 'No, darling, this definitely *isn't* 'Hiyas!' 'Hiyas!' is down the corridor.'

He receives party invitations from Hollywood box offices and regularly declines them. Elton John has issued several dinner invitations to no avail. But if one is vegan there is the ever-present danger of being photographed sat between a lobster salad and David Furnish. The American actor, Tom Hanks, once requested to meet him backstage after a concert in Los Angeles. A full, explanatory note was dispatched back to Mr Hanks:

'No.'

Had it been Ken Dodd, the Israeli actor Lior Ashkenazi or the late Doris Speed from *Coronation Street*, they would have been ushered through faster than a paramedic attending a prolapse.

This distancing is the necessary art of survival in an industry populated by itinerants with few basic skills, and characterised by sudden chart death followed by a deluge of friend petitions.

You do not remain at the top of the pyramid without developing the discerning nose of a sommelier. Other people will try to pass themselves off as a Chateau Margaux, to become your new best friend, but when one examines the execution of a hospitality rider they are soon revealed to be *vin ordinaire*. In this business, nothing may be taken for granted.

When Morrissey was still signed to Rough Trade, he was almost forced to occupy the roof of the record company in a protest to demand the backstage availability of scented candles, quality crudités and a private toilet, while the staff were booking holidays to Martinique on the back of *Hatful of Hollow* record royalties.

I have at times felt his acute loneliness and it is seemingly an unbridgeable emptiness. It is not diabetes or an insufficiently warmed-up fishcake in Carcassonne that will undo you (as it nearly did me), but loneliness. Loneliness can suffocate you with the sheer weight of hourly, if not *minutely*, desolation.

In a conversation that endeavoured to map the geometry of seclusion, I said, finally, 'I think you have to be more socially available.'

'What do you want me to do, hang above Henley-on-Thames in an air balloon?'

In the absence of a partner, I believe the stockpile of all that unspent love and desire has been, if not sublimated, discharged into the world as fusillades of epic biography.

But, it's not all Hebridean weather fronts stacking up and waiting to roll in to darken one's dawn. Morrissey bears his inner solitude manfully and, despite it, is rarely without that sabre-like sense of humour. Simply, he is the funniest person I have ever met.

As I write this, he is technically homeless and virtually lives on tour. Unbidden, because I'm a busybody who is unable not to interfere in the affairs of others, I tried to tempt him towards a variety of unusual or modern homes, and away from living in a gothic, Robert Bloch novel.

'And the beauty of it is, your existing furniture would give this particular space an interesting *tension* with absolutely no need to re-cover.'

'Tension?'

'Interest.'

'I can't sort tonight out, never mind remodel a windmill in Provence.'

'What about the bungalow on Crest Court, then?'

'I'm not going into a bungalow, it's far too OAP. Where is it?'

'Beverly Hills.'

'Well, it sounds like East Ham.'

It's not every day that someone offers to reform your group, put you on at the Royal Festival Hall and personally help with the buttering of the dinner rolls. Yet this is what happened in the June of 2004 when, after a thirty-year hiatus, Morrissey intervened in the New York Dolls and convinced David Johansen to splash out on a new silk blouse and fly to London.

Moreover, he invited me to support them with my collaborator Noko 440 in promotion of our 'Born That Way' single, released on the Attack label. This was truly an impossible fantasy come true. The Royal Festival Hall is, significantly, on my home turf of Bermondsey. Similarly, he asked them to play at the Move Festival in Old Trafford, within yards of the old house, after missing them in 1973 due to a heavy head cold.

For the setlist I toyed with the idea of opening with an a-cappella version of 'I've Written a Letter to Daddy', as performed by Baby Jane Hudson in that infamous piece of grand guignol *Whatever Happened to Baby Jane?* It appealed to me as a disturbing, knife-edge prelude—and one that could easily collapse into farce—before launching into the disciplined chaos of 'I'm Unbearable':

My provenance is South London '60 / I am a vinyl directive from Frankenstein / I begged my practitioner on Gucci knee / To pump a lethal prophylactic into my behind / Cheap, loud, recorded noise...

When the director of the festival telephoned me to ascertain the set order I said, 'I always begin with 'I've Written a Letter to Daddy'.'

'Of course,' he replied, matter-of-factly.

The problem with an unnatural tendency towards the oblique is that it can backfire and one has closed off any possibility of retreat. I was saved from myself due to an onstage time factor.

We went on to support Morrissey on the French and British leg of his 2005 *You Are the Quarry* tour, which became a slightly nerve-wracking affair as my collaborator, Noko, threatened to pull out several times. I cannot say I blamed him. Despite my underlined memos to the tour manager, Noko continued to remain invisible from both the marquee of the venue, its foyer and even from the dressing room door. He was convinced there was a behind-the-scenes conspiracy to eliminate him from any musical credit.

I should say that Morrissey was tolerant of my penchant for disregarding backstage regulations. I was always permitted to smoke next to a fire extinguisher, while watching the lighting rig go up, in what was a strictly carcinogenic-free zone for everybody else.

The after party at the Royal Festival Hall was memorable and its guests included Bob Geldof, Chrissie Hynde, Bobby Gillespie of Primal Scream and Jonathan Ross. For some reason, I confused Bob Geldof with Germaine Greer; from behind they look very similar, although I approached him from the front.

Simon Hoare, the drummer in both Raymonde and RPLA, who had enjoyed some success with his Victorian alter ego, Walter, on the Burlesque circuit, was circulating flyers to his upcoming show in the lobby and got locked out of the building. Simon so should have been at that party.

I spoke with both Sylvain Sylvain and Arthur Kane at some length before finally meeting David Johansen. David Johansen, the person unwittingly responsible for so much.

To meet one's hero is an occasion fraught with dilemma and difficulty. One either rambles on in near-hysteria like an adolescent schoolgirl, riding high on a tsunami of gushing compliments, or one is instantly struck mute. I think instinct told him who I was, because he looked at me as if I were the Eve Harrington character in *All About Eve*. The ambitious overstudy.

He proffered his hand, which I ignored, instead lurching forward to squeeze him in a bear hug—almost knocking the drink out of his hand—and kissed him full on the lips. Releasing him was a more complicated business because his hair got caught in the neck-chain of my tour laminate.

I was steered away from him by the elbows and guided towards the comparative safety of an international cheese board. Disastrous, but with one certain outcome: he'll remember me.

I saw him again in the dining marquee at the Move festival in Manchester, loudly scraping off an abandoned haddock from his plate into the catering bins with an expression of wan indifference. I thought it prudent not to approach. It never occurs to fans that the object of their worship might not be disposed to meet them.

Morrissey remains, for the greater part, an enigma. You may feel that you have peeled away the "mask", but beneath it lies another. You can try removing that one too, but it's pointless. To uncover the real Morrissey requires only to intently listen to the words.

In any case, nowadays, we are all so irretrievably steeped in our own status marquees and photo albums that mystique is an almost impossible prospect.

On fan worship, it is nice to be wanted and desirous to be loved, but it can depend on by whom. If you have attained any degree of notoriety or, less successfully, fame, you will discover that fervency and adoration can walk together with hateful piety and perceived betrayal. The devout greetings that avalanche into your inbox can unpredictably metamorphose into delirious scissor wielding at the stroke of an ill-advised B-side selection.

One returns home to find the cleaning lady slumped over the spin dryer in the first of a series of cloaked warnings, because your gatefold sleeve did not credit someone who waited vainly in a Pittsburgh downpour for a cancelled show.

I exaggerate, but fandom exaggerates even more. With his agreement, I once wrote to a Morrissey fan website forum under the pseudonym Abigail Lawson to point out that 'Little Man,

What Now?' was not, as popularly believed, a lyric about the British child actor Jack Wild. It is a circumstantial verse to the actor Malcolm McFee who appeared in the 1970s British television series, *Please Sir!* Abigail Lawson received no less than seventy-five death threats. Impressive.

Thus, one must take care to sidestep the rabid, mythological stampede of one's own zealots and, indeed, the forum cannibals who are a species best left to their own gnashing, circular idiocies. The latter are not fans; they are people who cry out for euthanasia.

The French philosopher Blaise Pascal once wrote: "The charm of fame is so great that we like every object to which it is attached, even death."

I would say, "*Especially* death."

My life has been enriched for having known and shared the friendship of such an absorbing, stimulating and, at times, compellingly awkward person. After thirty-two years, even I cannot quite figure him out. I no longer wish to.

It is an association that has nothing to do with Earl Grey tea, buttered crumpets or epigrams, but one founded upon a shared folk memory of a countercultural England that produced eccentricity, subversive genius and, in its finest moments, footwear radicalism.

It occurs to me only now that, following that telephone call so many autumns and hemline lengths ago, I might have been his very first fan.

ANNETTE, PLEASE CONTACT RECEPTION

GREEN HUNDRED ROAD. The name evokes the vision of a shady lane of wisteria hemmed by Tudorbethan homes; a dray horse delivering barrels of fine ale to the local hostelry, and the peculiarly English certainty that there must, and always will be, fresh homemade conserves.

Green Hundred Road, however, was situated in one of London's least desirable areas, and lined with 1930s-built tenements whose inhabitants were destined to fuel the future crack epidemic.

One never strolled down this street but instead trotted while looking both ahead and behind for potential assailants. This doesn't always work because the mugger, like the beloved velociraptor before him, often favours a rapid approach from the side. People are often so busy scanning the horizon that they don't know what's going on under their nose.

This is how people come to unknowingly have sex performed on them at a request bus stop.

Until Raymonde, my experience of the 1980s was somewhat limited to the aspect of a side window of my Peckham flat. This view was partially obscured by a long-dead tree with a torn, once-white plastic carrier bag caught perpetually in its seasonless branches. In other words, rather like my life.

I whiled away two whole years playing chess with a highly unpredictable gas boiler when not stood at a window that offered a scene of other people also economising on a state subsidy of £25 per week. I survived on tins of dolphin-unfriendly tuna. My cooking skills were non-existent: I could mismanage a cup of coffee.

Scouring popular culture as a means of life support, I used to board the number 12 bus for the hour's journey to Notting Hill to methodically re-file the racks of the Record & Tape Exchange. Here one could unearth obscure, rare and long since deleted records. Exotic labels, different textures, strange fonts. Records were like artefacts; you were an archaeologist and occasionally one would turn up something quite remarkable. In an age where the internet had yet to be invented, one had to be prepared to pound the pavement in order to find new inspiration.

The Gender Benders of the early 1980s together with the New Romantic movement hardly touched me, because although I liked the pseudo-fascist, ersatz glamour of it, the sound of synthesisers burying distorted voices that sang in black Chinese slippers did not seduce me. Those Chinese slippers really did beg to be stamped on.

So, you wouldn't find me at the Blitz Club or the Batcave in London's Soho, presided over by Steve Strange and the Queen of that movement, Siouxsie Sioux, dancing to Visage while affecting Weimar decadence in white face powder. I enjoyed Christopher Isherwood's Berlin diaries and the film *Cabaret*, but

I didn't see it as a lifestyle. Instead, I was at home reading William Burroughs in a fog of Gauloises and dancing to Serge Gainsbourg's 'Initials BB'.

Also, I had begun to properly discover cinema. At that time, one of the films that had made an impression on me was David Lynch's *Eraserhead*. I enjoy industrial landscapes and I feel at home in black & white. Similarly, I like Andrei Tarkovsky, particularly his meditation on faith, *Stalker*.

Eraserhead is a modern Gothic horror film. It is a film of very few comparisons whose origins quite possibly lie in the German cinema of the 1920s. The contrast is radiant light and stygian shadow; reality and dream are enmeshed and its themes are encoded. When it was released, I went to see it one winter afternoon in an unheated theatre close to Baker Street. We were an audience of two, me and a female student who had travelled from Hampshire. We chatted afterwards. She was messianic in her praise of the film, but compulsively peppered every sentence with the word "mega".

'That was mega-weird, wasn't it? I mean, really mega-dark.'

This habit was highly infectious because I, too, began sprinkling our short conversation with it. Immediately, she assumed that I was taking the piss out of her, shut up and went back to Basingstoke.

In a cruel twist of fate I saw her again, many years later, ahead of me in a check-in queue for a flight bound for Athens. She was at the counter, protesting at being charged an excess baggage fee and petitioning the clerk to waive it. 'But it's not *mega* overweight!' I imagined her saying.

The largest event, in every way, that I witnessed was when the fire brigade was called to the flat of a woman who lived in a neighbouring block. She was a single mother living with her three feral children, and who was known locally as The Fat Cow. Peckham shorthand lacks finesse. Obese to the point that she had become physically incapable of leaving the house, she was incarcerated— together with her self-adhesive dado rails—for the better part of a decade.

I'm an expert on incarceration and I feel that had she ventured to the front door a little more often, we might have struck up a dialogue in sign language. Regardless, her hair was so abundantly oily that had she risked the communal car park, she would have been immediately coned off as an environmental biohazard.

The story has it that while she was cooking in her galley kitchen she turned around and got wedged between the two work surfaces. Quite literally, she had to be cut out of her own fry-up. The emergency services managed to heave her onto a stretcher, which broke as they tried to load her into the ambulance, and into the gutter she fell.

As the jazz singer Cleo Laine is known for her multi-octave singing voice with incredible scatting ability, The Fat Cow possessed a similar talent with the word "cunt". Adolescent street muggers were stopped in their tracks as the air turned blue over the Friary Estate. And The Fat Cow passed into legend.

Another main event was the Greater London Council's plan to demolish a swathe of Peckham to make way for a high-speed rail link connecting the counties of Kent and Essex. I cannot fathom why commuters should want to get to their workplace more quickly, let alone be in a mad rush to get from Dartford to Barking; two lethally overcast dormitory towns without a sufficiently deep canal in which one might drown oneself.

An extraordinary meeting was called at the local Town Hall to which borough residents were invited to address their concerns to visiting government ministers. The hall was packed with an assortment of faces creased with anger and undiluted panic. I attended this civic meeting because even my indifference thought it important to know what the Council were going to do with me. In truth, I would have agreed to anything, including the seizing of all pet guinea pigs, if it meant a new maisonette with park views.

The discussion began reasonably enough with a civilised Q & A between tenants and a bespectacled, rumpled MP who coughed his way through a whole decanter of Volvic. Suddenly from the back of the hall came the long, teeth-clenching scraping of a chair. All heads swivelled through 180 degrees and towards the vision of Big Emmie rising to her great, slippered feet.

Big Emmie was the self-appointed, unofficial councillor of our constituency ward. Like great records, time stood still.

'*You*,' she roared at the panel in a voice that would have bulldozed Sir John Gielgud off the Theatre Royal stage, 'are *not* putting your *fucking* railway through my *fucking* backyard, alright?'

In those days, it seemed that everybody in Southwark ended their sentences with 'Al-*right*?', especially when in a heated argument. This is when they weren't having to physically turn round to speak with one another. 'So *I* turned round...then *she* turned round...so *I* turned round...'

All heads swivelled back towards the panel, who were stunned into silence.

'Right, that's sorted then. Bunch a'cunts.'

apartment. I'm not sure exactly as to what the Buenos Aires element might have been, but I painted the flat in black and white, which was very modern at the time, and bought a Yucca tree. Also, I bought a large, framed photograph of Helmut Newton's *Big Nude III*, which is my favourite photograph ever.

A friend once brought his girlfriend along and, confronted with my stroke at monochromatic minimalism, she had to lie down in the passage with all the lights turned off. However, she was Russian and I know they've been fighting for a bit of colour for years.

My stint at the Labour Party HQ ended shortly after attending their Christmas Party. I decided to wear a suit, shirt and tie with a nice pair of black patent court shoes. I've never relied on the excuse of an annual Charity Fun Day to slip into a pair of heels.

I was standing at the buffet table eating an *amuse bouche* and earwigging Margaret Beckett who, apparently, enjoys caravan holidays. A freelance photographer friend of mine was assigned to a photoshoot of Margaret Beckett and was instructed to make her look "attractive and appealing". That effort almost destroyed her desire to develop anything.

While I was pouring myself another glass of Champagne, Michael Foot, who was then the Leader of the Opposition, asked to cross by to help himself to a state subsidised vol-au-vent. He was under enormous strain at the time because the leadership of his party had splintered away to form a faction who called themselves the Social Democrats. This, when he wasn't being borne down upon by that lacquered *convoi exceptionnel*, Margaret Thatcher, in the Houses of Parliament.

Momentarily, looking down at my feet he commented:

'Nice shoes.'

'Thank you. How's it going?'

'Oh, you know.'

'You must be under an awful lot of pressure.'

'Well...'

'You should try fly fishing. Apparently, it's very relaxing. Do you have a pair of waders?'

He fled.

THE PARLOUR OF
MAITRESSE DESCLAVES

FOR THE FIRST HALF-DECADE of the 1980s, sex contrived
to evade my life's radar. There might have been the odd blip,
and then it was gone. Why this should have been so is a little
intriguing given that I didn't convincingly resemble the rear of
a bus replacement service to East Sheen.

Also, I was fairly outgoing and made a considerable effort to
be amenable. Friendly, even. This elicited sympathetic looks
from the chatty, prolapsed checkout girl at my local mini-market.

'Any?'

'No.'

'Something will crop up, babes.'

'You've just swiped through that Devon Ambrosia Custard
twice.'

In writing this account I had imagined that in not alluding to
the lascivious details of my intimate life I would spare the reader
any inessential discomfort. In fact, to withhold these particulars
might provide this book with a unique selling point in a world
already vividly crammed with carnal detail. Besides, nobody is
interested in reading about sex unless it involves either celebrities or zoophilia. Although, celebrity sex *is* a form of zoophilia.

Up until I met my partner, my intimate life could best be described, in both scale and lack of feature, as Namibian. Friends sometimes assumed that I was a kind of sexual avenger who plotted a course of liaison with other people's brothers and fathers, converging on their existences like a misdirected Doctor Crippen.

This is only partly true. I lived without sex for quite a long time. It is not easy to live without such pleasures for a prolonged time unless one can sublimate it with community work, a consuming hobby or, if you're desperate, poetry.

One begins to implode, subconsciously embarking upon the descent into minutiae and mortal danger. The choreography of the extreme prevails as one begins to follow soap operas, arguing back at their characters. One becomes stitched to obsession because compulsiveness is what we have in place of a relationship with someone other than ourselves.

When life deprives us of this realm, either the decision is made to have life all for ourselves—which is spinsterhood made to look like election rather than inevitability—or we apply to become an outreach worker.

Again, it is loneliness that kills, not high-fat spreads and Brandy Alexanders.

Rarely have I ever been capable of simply enjoying a record, a film or a book. When something inspires me it immediately becomes an addiction. I'll excavate it to the point of exhaustion, until there is nothing more that I can possibly glean from it.

The interlude at that time was generally filled by anything produced by ITC Entertainment between 1967 and 1970. I passed many an afternoon with Peter Wyngarde. Wyngarde is a much unacknowledged actor. His performances in the sci-fi espionage series *Department S*, before being assigned his own series in *Jason King*, were seamless and masterful and as good as anything you'll see at the Royal Court. A novelist and part-time crime fighter, his character would jet around Europe's playgrounds, the cravat ever-present, constantly replenishing a cigarette holder while dining at Michelin-starred restaurants and saying "*Fancy*" quite a lot.

Menton, Cadenabbia, Gstaad. This glamour mesmerised me.

A female friend of mine, whom I will call Patricia, because indeed that is her name, was a handsome woman in the style of a film noir femme fatale who worked as a receptionist in an upscale brothel. This brothel catered exclusively to men wishing to actualise their fetishist fantasies before, no doubt, returning to a disconsolate wife, an endowment mortgage, and a daughter whose orthodontics billing had eclipsed any possibility of a summer holiday.

She suggested not that I turn to prostitution as a means of acquiring physical contact—prostitution is the opposite of pro-pinquity—but rather that considering my track record, I wasn't perhaps cut out to be a gay man and should instead look towards an alternative expression of sexuality. I thought this quite original and radical of her.

'There's loads of men out there who love a bit of domination, you know.'

'But what would I have to do?'

'You can do exactly what you want. You're quite bossy, you might enjoy it.'

She put a finger to her lips.

'Eva, I think.'

'Eva?'

'It's a wig in Kensington Market. Good starter wig. Perfect for you.'

Standing before a full-length, guilt-framed mirror in her dressing room, poured into a black latex catsuit, shoehorned into a pair of high-heeled thigh boots and with "Eva" in place, I was transformed into six feet and two inches of neoprene intent. Not unreasonable to say that the effect was rather Helmut Newton. It was a visual revelation, and I should say that I was quite taken with myself.

'*Fancy.*'

I sat down on the chaise longue and lit a Dunhill while Patricia busily backcombed one of her many stylistic creations.

'Tu as été un garçon très désobéissant...'

'Oh, now that *is* nice. Very nice. See, you're getting the hang of it already?' she offered, whilst rectifying a ringlet.

'You'll need a name, of course. Something French, because I see you can get away with it.'

The faux-suede parlour of Maitresse Desclaves was simple yet comfortable. There was a slender walnut desk, a large mirror with an ornate frame, a leather reading chair and a sofa; all purchased at discount from a secondhand furniture shop in Wandsworth called *Steptoe and Mum*. I had grown tired of "Buenos Aires" and was now residing in "Bir Hakeim, Paris".

I had just seen Nathalie Delon in *Ils s'appellent ça un accident* and had fallen in love with her. Or, rather, her cape.

Various accountants and telesales executives dusted and

polished that walnut table to a state of high finish and took care of my laundry. There are certain men who, under pressure in their work and in their personal lives, throw themselves into a convulsion of detergent—and under the spiked heels of a callously indifferent authority figure—to unburden themselves of accumulated stress. So, in one sense, I had gone into community service.

'I know you're not charging but it's expected of them to bring a gift, a tribute,' said Patricia one eventless, drizzling Thursday afternoon that Lambeth excels at.

'Well, it's true, I could do with a new wok.'

BDSM is a mystery to many people but then some people prefer to play ping pong, bowling or bingo which, to me, is more deeply perverse. The word "dominatrix" typically conjures up the image of the archetypal bitch with a whip. Untrue. The roleplay that had resuscitated my sex life interested me for the aspect of a relationship played out through fantasy and imagination. There is an intellectual component in those explorative scenarios where trust is always implicit.

In the sexual star system, it is at the other end of the galaxy to what might be termed a "straight fuck". There is much to be said for a straight fuck, of course, but that opportunity had been lacking in my life, otherwise I would not have arrived here.

I explored the realm of sensual domination. Thrashing somebody to within an inch of the cottage hospital with a family heirloom didn't appeal to me, it is not my style, as neither were pain-hungry submissives.

The whisper is more effective than the command, as Schubert can be more unsettling than any Norwegian death metal record.

A brushing against the skin can be erotic and memorable in a way that the seizing hand is diminished by its force. Perfume lingers longer than the weal.

Remarkably, I had travelled swiftly from being an involutary celibate to having a variety of attractive heterosexual men at my feet, and on my terms. This is the fantasy of many gay men. And quite a few women, too. Additionally, I amassed a collection of top of the range, German-made kitchen utensils, which is not to be sniffed at.

Only once was there a mishap. There was an episode when I ordered a submissive haulage contractor to apply Tiger Balm to his testicles and run a milk errand for me while I read Sartre's *No Exit*. I suppose this might be an adult progression of those games of kindling intrigue many years before with Cherelle. He did my bidding but, unfortunately, the electrical wiring in the main security door had short-circuited, necessitating a lengthy wait until a resident left the building.

On returning, he was visibly flushed and in a state of considerable discomfort, if not anguish.

'What's my wife going to say when she sees this?' he implored.

A rather bald statement, I thought. I turned a page.

'What's your wife's name?'

'Yvonne, Maitresse.'

'Would you like me to telephone…what's her name again?'

'*Yvonne*, Maitresse.'

The Tiger Balm was now at Def Con 5.

'I can explain to…*Yvette*, is it?'

'No, Maitresse.'

I placed a bookmark at a new chapter.

'Good. Stick your balls in the sink and then go away quickly. You're dismissed.'

'Yes, Maitresse.'

I enjoyed my brief foray into the world of Maitresse Desclaves, not least because it was a voyage of discovery, giving me a rare insight into human nature while also delivering me from the tedium of domestic chores.

Significantly, it equipped me with the skills required to deal with musicians later in life.

CODA

NOT LONG AFTER DESPATCHING "EVA" down the communal rubbish chute I met my life partner, Paul. The Polar Bear. The Dane. I am blessed by the love, the tenderness and the support of a steadfast friend, a broad set of shoulders and a life partner. This is the real success of my life. Simply, he is a good man. He has faith in me and restores my confidence when I have felt dispirited, if not lost.

Love. Unconditional. Ultimately unquantifiable. We have shared many adventures together. Contrary to my track record, for me life is enhanced through the act of sharing, because it amplifies yet distils those moments of joy, discovery and laughter.

If we're lucky we may occasionally experience wonder. But laughter is terribly important. When you cease to laugh together, or laugh alone, something has indeed died. Human relationships can be impossibly complex at times, and there is a myriad of reasons why some partnerships may last twenty years and others only twenty minutes.

Chemistry, of course, is fundamental because after the initial honeymoon period one may go directly to picking up discarded socks. The small sacrifices that domesticity brings: some protest, make an illogical fuss and even dissolve a shared bank account rather than yield to the tea towel. Others know that fabric conditioner is a fact of life and, accordingly, adjust to reality.

I understand that some people prefer the world all to themselves. To not confuse happiness with one particular person is an intelligent decision, and possibly the secret to contentment. Ultimately, we must not rely on other people to make us happy; it is not their responsibility.

From the moment one falls in love, one embarks upon six months of indescribable torment: one sees beauty in everything and is always ever so slightly out of breath. Being in love is not unlike being a hostage to a musical in which one breaks off in the middle of dialogue to sit by a window, singing a love poem to a Clerkenwell pigeon. This is what love does to us.

I have no idea where I would be now, or how my life might have been had I not met Paul. Although I suspect that without the love and support of such an unselfish partner—stoic, even—I would now probably be emotionally shutdown. Dribbling slightly. Perhaps piecing together a jigsaw puzzle depicting the Bernese Oberland in a hostel in Peacehaven.

Certainly, I shouldn't imagine I'd be sitting here in turquoise, writing this up. Living with me has, on occasion, consisted of living with a variety of characters, not all of whom you'd wish to meet.

Thank you, Paul.

THE SENTINEL OF STUDHOLME STREET

I DECIDED THAT I HAD BETTER do something other than correspond with other library ticket fine holders and crippled bedroom casualties. My relationships were entrenched in notepaper, manila and the correct stampage. Metaphorically, my hair was creeping towards a French Pleat.

I once wrote to the British comedy actress Hylda Baker offering to set up an appreciation society in her honour. Unbeknownst to me, she was installed at The Entertainment Artist's Benevolent Home in Twickenham where she fell into an enviable coma from which she never awoke. In a sense, I was relieved that there was no reply because I'm not quite sure what I would have filled the newsletter with.

At the time, I had a friend, Lyndsay, whom I met through her former boyfriend Kevin who ran a secondhand clothes stall at Camden Market. Lyndsay was the undisputed Brigitte Bardot of Peckham. She was handsome, sexy, self-assured and rode a Triumph motorbike. She had waist-length hair, thick and glossy, an hourglass figure, height and direct eye contact. Unsurprisingly, she had no female friends.

Lyndsay was fearless. If she knew that you were attracted to her she would mischievously tease you to the point of mute frustration, although always with a twinkle in the eye. She left Kevin—who was a big-boned Cheshire lad who wore clothes not dissimilar to Diana Rigg in *The Avengers*—after she stumbled across a photograph album of holiday snaps that featured all her predecessors. As she flipped back through the cellophaned years, her intestines unravelled and re-knotted themselves at the horror of a Kodak gallery displaying her "doppelgangers", all standing by the same bilingual road sign in Snowdonia, pointing and laughing.

We would take the bus to King's Cross, often to the gay pub venue called The Bell, to threaten the DJ with a long-stemmed comb into playing The Birthday Party, when all that anyone wanted to hear was Hi-NRG. It occurred to me that quite a lot of gay men shared identical music tastes as thirteen-year-old girls; it's virtually the same demographic market. Hi-NRG was like a Trojan that spread exponentially. In the manner of *The Invasion of the Body Snatchers*, a dear friend might be reborn overnight as an Evelyn Thomas fan. Moreover, it happened to the people one most cherished.

Before she swapped her Vauxhall for a motorbike, we found an opened bank security box by the kerb on Catlin Street as we were walking to her car. It contained £150 and some documents. Seemingly, it had been thrown from a vehicle after a robbery. We were about to divide the money between us when we saw a police car approaching. Lyndsay jumped into her car and put the box under the driver's seat. I slid into the passenger seat and, seeing a police officer in the rear mirror, immediately feigned a violent headache.

'Is this your car, madam?'

'Yes, I'm just taking my friend to hospital.'

'What seems to be the problem, sir?'

'Meningitis.'

'Meningitis?'

'Well, it *could* be.'

'Diana Dors has got it,' Lyndsay chimed in with undue corroboration.

He was deliberating whether to order us out of the vehicle. Suddenly his radio twittered and, for an instant, he turned his back. Lyndsay swung the car into reverse and we hurtled around the corner into oncoming traffic. We spent our windfall at Camden Market; we bought matching black and white polka dot shirts.

It was she who suggested I try to find some musicians to work with. A pattern emerges: as with Patricia, handsome women advise me and I follow their instructions implicitly.

I saw an advertisement for a singer in the *New Musical Express*. They were a duo. They cited their influence as Joy Division and, conveniently for me, their telephone prefix was the same as mine. In fact, I had only to walk to a house at the very end of my street for the audition.

Paul H. played synthesiser and Eamonn played the bass guitar. They used a drum machine. Paul was very thin and pale with a skin tone of ghost-white verging on lavender. He had long, manicured nails and was tightly clad in black. I suppose you might have called him a proto-Goth, although I doubt he would have appreciated it. Paul had a succession of girlfriends, one of whom endearingly reminded me of a young Adrienne Posta. Her predecessor was from Balham and was always complaining that someone had put salt on her chips.

'Why is there salt on my fucking chips?'

'I do wish you wouldn't swear, it's so disempowering.'

'Fuck off.'

Eamonn, the bass player, doesn't really merit description.

The audition itself comprised a chit-chat about Factory Records' cover design, the ascertaining of the width of my drainpipes, and a mutual astonishment that we both shopped at Minimarket Tina without ever having crossed paths. I suppose that if your name is Tina, and you run a minimarket, why call it anything else?

The group already had an existing name: Chi-Rho. Chi-Rho is one of the earliest cruciform symbols used by Christians and is formed by superimposing the first two letters of Christ in Greek. I disliked it intensely. I thought it sounded like a street in Taiwan and suggested we change the name to The Third Sex.

The Third Sex made only one appearance, a few months later, at a local community centre to which we invited everyone we knew. We played five songs whose composition and style was influenced by Joy Division and Nico's *Drama of Exile*. It was my first ever gig. After the performance, Eamonn left the group for a job in the financial district that offered a subsidised canteen and private medical insurance.

These were the very first songs that I wrote, and yet I can scarcely remember the titles. Perhaps it's selective amnesia. I recall that the leading instrument, the synthesiser, with its hollow, anodyne insistence began to wear me down rather, and soon I longed for the more organic, lush and warm sound of guitars. This is not a criticism of Paul H.; I simply preferred the latter to the former.

Paul resisted the idea of incorporating a guitarist, thinking, quite rightly, that he might be usurped in the song writing duties. Eventually, it was to be proven. After much discussion, and at my strongest urging, we placed an advertisement in the *New Musical Express* for a guitarist. That guitarist was to be Phil Huish with whom I formed Raymonde.

The house in which Paul lived, he shared with his mother. He occupied a sort of flatlet at the back of the house with a kitchenette, a sitting room and a bedroom. The window overlooked the garden, which might once have been pleasant to sit in, but which was now little more than a yard for the dog's toiletry. The side window overlooked the houses on Studholme Street where, later, I was to live for awhile.

Often, at night-time, one could discern the unmoving silhouette of a woman sat at a window, looking out from beneath an unshaded lightbulb. We called her The Sentinel. There are seven sentinels who guard the seven portals to other dimensions, and I can semi-reliably inform you that one of them is positioned directly above 6 Studholme Street in Peckham.

Paul's mother was a good person, albeit a lonely one, until she discovered, in sequence, the St John's Ambulance, the Territorial Army—in which she rose to the rank of Second Lieutenant—and the local Conservative Party. Given the neighbourhood, the latter could have all convened in a modest conservatory. She was a staunch supporter of the "Iron Lady", Margaret Thatcher, which grated at Paul's socialist ideals; he sometimes winced even on hearing his mother's footsteps doggedly climb the stairs to the shared bathroom.

There existed between them a brittle peace that could ignite into warfare at the slightest domestic grievance. However, such was her solitude, and her curiosity at finding a mildly interesting stranger in the house, that she began to climb the stairs more often to seek some company. This became a regular feature of my visits and we'd talk airily of this and that whilst her son visibly closed down next to the water boiler. She might have been broad-hipped, but she was certainly broadminded. I liked her.

The final straw came one winter's morning when it was still dark outside. Mrs H. was preparing to go to work at her job as a civil servant with the local Job Centre. Seeing a pile of dog faeces in the middle of the kitchen floor, and running late, she decided to leave it there until she returned home. Importantly, the wall switch to the fluorescent lighting strip was positioned not at the door but at the far end of the kitchen.

By six o'clock in the evening, the sun had already set and it was nightfall. On coming home, she advanced into the kitchen to turn on the light. Paul H. and I were upstairs discussing Edith Piaf when the floor vibrated with a plaster-cracking thump followed by the din of crashing pans.

Five minutes later came footsteps ascending the stairs, this time a little heavier and slower than usual. There was a knock at the door, but instead of the customary sharp rap it was more of a pendulous address, such as that of a ghost returning to unnerve new tenants. The door handle turned with meek purchase, uncertain at first. Then the door slowly creaked wide open to reveal the Dame of Peckham, as she was later knighted, standing there with an expression of crushing petition, cradling her elbow with her right hand.

'Do you think you could make me a cup of coffee? Only I think I've broken my arm?'

We parted company shortly after. Paul left home, after which he enjoyed a much better relationship with his mother, and went to work in the travel industry. He moved to leafier Sydenham and shared a house with an older, gay man. Paul's sexual orientation was heterosexual, yet he became the recipient of numerous, feverish missives slipped under his bedroom door at an hour when most normal people would be in bed: '50 Reasons Why I Love Paul'.

And I ran away, for which it took years to be forgiven, with our new guitarist.

RAYMONDE

"AND DO YOU STILL WEAR that biker jacket with RAYMONDE on?" I sang upon entering a vocal booth for the very first time.

Raymonde saved my life. If I had not met Phil Huish, my collaborator and Raymonde's guitarist, it is almost certain that I would have chained myself to the railings outside 10 Downing Street in a bid to splash myself across the front of *Jackie* magazine.

Phil Huish was a tough little man and as Cockney as they come. Mischievous, with a sense of humour that masked hidden complexes, he had already been hauled before the juvenile courts for stealing a power drill from Woolworth's. Excellent credentials. He was born into a large clan of sisters and brothers from Herne Hill in South London, all of whom deferred to the diminutive matriarch of Mrs Huish.

Mrs Huish decided that she liked me, which was nice because not many people did, and on forming Raymonde I was often invited to join the family for supper. One dared not leave anything on the plate, including the cutlery. They were a good-natured lot. They would argue yet laugh minutes later; they were loud — doors were never closed but slammed; and they seemed to accept me unconditionally.

These suppers could be slightly surreal in that the conversation might oscillate between Millwall Football Club's chances of advancing to the Second Division, Mrs Huish's account of how she personally removed a drunkard from her workplace, the Crusty Cob bakers, and concern over one of the daughters who was stranded in the Great Socialist People's Libyan Arab Jamahiriya.

Phil had a girlfriend. A childhood sweetheart with bomb-proof hair called Julie. We were introduced in what proved to be a fleeting, first and last encounter. For some reason, she took an instant dislike to me, which was a pity because Phil and I began to spend a large amount of time together, leaving her at home to rearrange her Carmen rollers. Later, she too was "removed", not by Mrs Huish but by the arrival of a new girlfriend.

Our collaboration was prolific. In the space of a little under three years we wrote close to sixty songs, many of which were unrecorded. We recruited a drummer Leslie Westlake, who was all of nineteen, and Gary Bainbridge as the bass player. He was a barrel-chested, South Shields construction worker newly settled in London. Both were later replaced by Derek Thompson on bass and Simon Hoare who went on to become percussionist with RPLA.

We produced a 4-track demo titled *Nothing Stops Here* and distributed it, plundering the telephone directory to secure live dates. Our first concerts were at the pub and live music venue The Half Moon in Herne Hill. This led to shows at the cavernous Boston Arms in Tufnell Park and, notably, The Rock

Garden in London's West End.

After a performance at The Rock Garden we were approached by Mike Alway, an A & R representative for Cherry Red Records and manager of his own label, él Records. Alway was an eccentric and nonconformist; a pop conceptualist from Brentford in West London who, it struck me, was far too talented to be working in the music industry.

He was also very much an Englishman. An ex-art student with a penchant for late medieval imagery, he was a charming style gourmand given to strident pronouncements. As I came off stage he greeted me with open arms and said, 'Bassey!'

I thought, 'This is the person we are going to sign with.'

Phil and I made several trips out to his Barnes home, which looked as if it had been shortly vacated by Ian Carmichael, to design the sleeve for our debut single 'I'll Light a Candle'. It appealed to me that, in Mike Always' rococo world, designing the sleeve was deemed far more of a priority than recording the song. Moreover, Alway created artists who, to all intents and purposes, did not really exist outside of his imaginative and lovingly rendered cover art.

Ultimately, the project with él Records never came to fruition because we were served, by the Cherry Red organisation which owned it, a full and binding contract for recording and publishing rights in which there was no fiscal advance for this or any future product.

Phil and I needed to be able to concentrate fully on Raymonde and we were seeking a modest retainer to live on; just enough to keep the gas connected and a weekly case of Fitou for me.

As we continued to play live we began to attract press attention and were invited to an interview with the *New Musical Express*. At this point, Martin Sexton, a publishing gunslinger from Fiction Records, which was effectively The Cure's own label, bounded into my life. He telephoned me and whisked me off to Brighton to meet the writer Jim Shelley with whom I struck up an acquaintanceship. Shelley was then a music journalist but is now a television columnist for a British tabloid newspaper. Soon after, we played in Brighton to an audience and Brett Anderson.

Sexton was a large and effusive Anglo-Irishman who loved glamour—an element distinctly lacking in the shoe-gazing Indiedom of 1985—and was drawn to Raymonde. His real passion was for photography and painting, rather than music. A worrying pattern emerged in that we seemed to appeal to people who weren't terribly interested in music.

We signed a publishing deal with Fiction on the proviso that they release our debut single, 'Raymonde', which we had recently recorded and preferred to the song, 'I'll Light a Candle'. The ink on the contract was barely dry before, while giving an interview to *The Face* magazine, I referred to Robert Smith of The Cure as "a fat bitch". This rather put a dampener on the Fiction Records Christmas party, somewhat spoiling the family atmosphere. Apart from The Cure and Raymonde, the only other artist signed to their publishing roster was the enigmatic Billy Mackenzie.

Fiction Records was situated in Ivor Grove, next door to a Lebanese restaurant run by the formidable Fatima who produced the best falafel sandwiches in London. This is where we held our board meetings and I once whiled away an afternoon there with Billy Mackenzie.

The Associates knew the essence of glamour and enjoyed considerable chart success in the early 1980s. Billy's voice is the Cubby Broccoli *James Bond* theme song that should have been, but was never recorded. His range was startling. Our acquaintanceship was only brief but it was memorable. The trappings of pop success seemingly left no mark on him and the sojourns from his home in Dundee to London were interludes that stole him away from his other passion, the rearing of whippets.

I once sent him a letter and, in return, received a partly-torn photograph of a whippet. I forget the short text that accompanied it, but I doubt that it might have any further illuminated one.

Billy committed suicide in 1997 shortly after the death of his mother. Both Siouxsie Sioux and Robert Smith wrote elegies to Billy with 'Say' and 'Cut Here' respectively. It is rumoured that The Smiths' 'William, It Was Really Nothing' was written about him, but I do not know if this is true.

In the January of 1986, we graced the cover of *Melody Maker*. Reading it recently, the interview is breathtakingly arrogant, even haughty, and roundly dismissive of the then current musical topography. But the claims and the barbs are also the passion and the revenge of someone who was kept in a low, dark cupboard under the stairs for too many years, and who was now free to occupy centre stage. Even if only momentarily.

'Raymonde' was released and entered the Independent charts at number 20. At that time, the music press, with a sizeable national readership, held considerable sway and its writers could make or break an artist. If you were not liked, your prospects were slim. There was a fierce rivalry between *Melody Maker* and *New Musical Express*, or The Enemy, who had initially discovered us and had now assumed an unfavourable stance on Raymonde.

I'm quite used to this. My standard reaction to a negative review is to consume chocolate while flicking through a holiday brochure. It's a wonder that I'm not enormous. Retrospectively, one derives a little satisfaction in the probability that the latter rag swerves in and out of receivership and wields all the power of a maiden aunt who cannot leave the commode.

Sounds, the other paper in the triumvirate of popular British music press, could not decide whether to feature Raymonde or the techno-tranny phenomenon of the rapidly rising Sigue Sigue Sputnik—both groups having risen without trace—and so we shared the front page. Tony James, the guitarist in Sigue Sigue Sputnik is, I feel, an interesting person and it is a strange accident that we have never met.

Not long after the release of the 'Raymonde' single, a deal was negotiated with Geoff Travis' Blue Guitar label, an offshoot of Chrysalis Records, to record our album. Geoff Travis certainly had a full dinner plate with an overloaded roster at his own independent label Rough Trade.

Notwithstanding the meteoric success of The Smiths, he ran another label in Blanco y Negro which belonged to Warners. How he had the time to ride to and from work, in notoriously congested London traffic, on his tricycle is a mystery of time and motion.

Babelogue was recorded with Mark Saunders as engineer and David M. Allen producing, right at the end of the Northern Line in the compulsively clipped hedgerows of suburban

Wimbledon. Saunders was the more suitable choice, as he was a better engineer for this project than Allen as producer.

Derek Thompson had left Raymonde to go and do some tape-looping with Hoodlum Priest, so Peter Thomas came aboard as bass player. Peter was a perfect addition to the complement and to the sound of the group, which had temporarily derailed through Thompson's open-fret thumping. He was musicianly, companionable and almost absurdly decent, especially when you put him up against me.

During the recording of 'Sex, Love, Security' which, inadvisably, I began singing after a long and heavy lunch with Allen, my vocal pitch was a little out-of-kilter. I compensated by opening another bottle of Bordeaux. At vocal take number twelve, I disrobed. I insisted, through the intercom system, that someone come into the vocal booth and fellate me, *en même temps chantant*, to achieve the effect I was striving for.

Understandably, the control room broke out in a rustle of sudden and unusually close interest in the day's events as reported by the *Wimbledon Post*. Admittedly, my judgement was impaired and I announced that I had no intention of leaving the vocal booth until the take was in the can.

There followed an indecorous episode where I insulted everyone within sight, the studio management and Wimbledon in general while Phil pushed me through an exit sign and folded me into a waiting taxi.

Otherwise, the recording of *Babelogue* went smoothly and without any further incident. Geoff Travis visited the studio to check on our progress on a couple of occasions and, as I later learned, confided his misgivings to Morrissey.

Travis: 'There's a problem. James can't sing.'

Morrissey: 'Geoff, you're missing the point.'

Two weeks later...

Travis: 'There's a problem. James has designed a not very attractive sleeve for the album.'

Morrissey: 'Geoff, you're missing the point.'

One week later...

Travis: 'I love the Raymonde album! It's very 1960s.'

Morrissey: 'Geoff, you're missing the point.'

Prior to the release of *Babelogue,* we recorded four session tracks for the Janice Long radio show at the BBC. We were invited again to record a further session of newly written tracks that were slated for a possible second album. Also, a free flexi-single including the track *Jennifer Wants* was distributed with copies of the *Record Mirror.*

I appreciate *Babelogue* more as the years have passed. It is an ambitious album in that there is no specific anchor to the musical style. It moves from the upbeat, arpeggio power pop of 'No One Can Hold a Candle to You'—later re-recorded for the B-side of Morrissey's 'I Have Forgiven Jesus' single—to the conflagrant swamp rock of 'The Milk Train Doesn't Stop Here Anymore', the Bowie-inspired 'Been Too Many Years' and on to the mock aria of 'Oh Hellish Choir!'

"The cloak of fatigue falls upon thy breast!"

What on earth was I thinking? Or, perhaps, drinking?

In this sense, the album was not as "listener friendly" as many other independent offerings at the time. From the opening chords of the first track, you cannot necessarily forecast what lay in store ahead of the fizzling feedback of the closer.

There was a good deal of lazy and fatiguing journalistic comparisons that insisted Raymonde were very much like The Smiths. This developed more from the fact of my association with Morrissey, which was popular knowledge, rather than being founded in true, musical fact. It was journalists who were obsessed with The Smiths, not Raymonde, and there are other groups who are more deserving of that similitude.

I could have dressed up as Pearl Bailey and sang in an all-black production of *Hello Dolly!* and the review still would have claimed me as a "Smiths copyist". Many people attending our live shows came away believing differently and that was enough for me.

Raymonde supported The Smiths on a nationwide tour in support of the *Queen Is Dead* album. Two concerts stand out. One was at Salford University, where the breath and perspiration of the capacity audience was so abundant that it fell as rain from the rafters, together with crowd noise that caused distress to the ceiling of the venue.

The other was St Austell in Cornwall. We were having a party in our dressing room when I heard 'Bigmouth Strikes Again' over the tannoy. I loved this song. Thus, I immediately made direct course for the stage, nonchalantly waltzing past security in my knickers, and joined them. It was a spontaneous, impetuous act inspired by youthful excitement. And Bordeaux, again.

The next day I received a message in the form of a paperback novel delivered through the tour manager: Agatha Christie's *Murder Is Easy*. From then on, I had the distinct feeling of being under surveillance during their set. Trouble Maker.

The tour ended at the London Palladium where, receiving mild applause at the end of the concert, I announced 'Thank you. *You ignorant bastards.*'

And flounced off.

Two singles were culled from the *Babelogue* album. 'Stop Kicking My Heart Around' and 'Solid State Soul'. 'Solid State Soul' reduced me almost to tears. Not because I was unhappy with the hi-hat, but because the itinerant in charge of the art department at Chrysalis had mined new depths of ineptitude. The single sleeve is amongst the simplest of designs ever to be crayoned. It was a block colour selected from a Pantone chart with the song title in large, 32-point EdnaBold font. They pressed it, without my prior approval, in completely the wrong colour. One would need to be a wilful imbecile with liquorice-stained lips to mismanage such a task.

There is a clip of Nico in Philippe Garrel's 1972 film, *La Cicatrice Intérieure* (The Inner Scar) where she traipses through the sand dunes, moaning and crying like a misery guts, eventually plonking herself down to await death.

When I saw the aforementioned single sleeve, I reacted the same.

Babelogue sold moderately well, despite the fact that few people even knew it had been released, because there was no publicity or promotional plan for the album. Any publicity afforded us was by virtue of a postgraduate sub-editor taking an interest in my eccentricity. We were now being managed, under an unsigned contract, by Cerne Channing, who later managed Franz Ferdinand.

Inexplicably, after supporting The Smiths we were attached to a bill with proto-Goth outfit The Bolshoi, which is akin to pairing Marlene Dietrich with Arthur Mullard. Interesting perhaps, but ludicrous. Transparently, we were playing to the wrong hairstyles.

I came onstage to a sea of Robert Smith doppelgangers. Revenge, obviously, for my earlier insult. There was a fashion for beer throwing at these concerts and Phil began to carry a weapon on stage.

'Can we be optimistic and say that we shan't be needing that?'

'If any cunt throws anything...'

'Yes, but you can't take a small pick-axe on stage with you, darling.'

The front sleeve of 'Stop Kicking My Heart Around' is a photograph of him taken seconds before driving the sharp end of his Fender Telecaster into a wearisome student's face. On one occasion, at a concert given in London, a beer artist and heckler was set upon by two of Phil's brothers who happened to be in the stalls. He was kicked until unconscious and the set had to be stopped while the paramedics were called to the scene.

In Belfast, what appeared to be a small bomb package was tossed onto the stage, which I rather expertly kicked back into the dress circle with a black patent slipper. In Dublin, I wandered too far downstage and suddenly disappeared from view, falling ten feet into a concrete pit. As no one thought to rescue me I was obliged to deliver the rest of the concert whilst peeking over a barricade.

The accommodations became worse as the whole affair began to visibly disintegrate, reaching its nadir at a guest house in Dundee. You could not even have contemplated walking barefoot on the linoleum. The bedding was so highly flammable and soiled that one was obliged to sleep in an overcoat.

On check-out, Phil removed the side drawer of a dressing table and went into the communal bathroom. After a few minutes, he returned and neatly slid the drawer back into place. As we left I inched it open. He had left the next wretched guest a very personal souvenir, although I'm sure it could hardly have elicited shock given the surroundings.

I think this comes under the classification of "jape".

My twenty-sixth birthday fell at the next stop in Glasgow. Our tour manager, who was of no fixed address since he didn't need one, having been on the road since 1968 with the ubiquitous John Mayall (in every rehearsal studio in England you will see an instrument case with "John Mayall" stencilled on it) decided to arrange a birthday present for me.

While no doubt coming from a kind place, I do wish people would at least make a little investigation into one's fancies before choreographing a surprise. A surprise when ill-conceived can come off as assault.

There was a faint knock on my bedroom door and when I opened it there stood a teenaged girl with a shaven head and, I soon divined, when she said 'Hi', a missing front tooth. I didn't have the heart to close the door on her and so invited her in. We spent the next three hours discussing her alcohol abuse problem.

Enough is too much. Unwilling to continue with this charade, I informed everybody that I was taking the next train back to London. Back to Peckham. And back to Mrs Minkin at the Unemployment Bureau.

Chrysalis Records released us from the Blue Guitar label and our association with Geoff Travis effectively ended.

In 1987, following the disbandment of The Smiths, Morrissey took a holiday to Los Angeles and suggested that I accompany him. My savings account with the Co-Operative Bank had dwindled to a sum considerably below that which a modestly well behaved child might expect from Santa. Geoff Travis, who very much wanted to retain Morrissey in some way, advanced me the air fare and booked me a suite at Le Parc in West Hollywood.

Two weeks later, I returned home to the frantically blinking light of my answerphone. Regrettably, you do not send someone to the unemployment line and then make fiscal requests of them via an unreliable answering service.

Raymonde went into stasis and I worked at yet another temporary position, this time with the Town Hall in Southwark. As far as office work goes it was undemanding. They were quite flexible with me, and I took every opportunity to absent myself.

My boss was in a pharmaceutical daze for most of the time because he was addicted to suppositories. He was usually to be found in the toilets, pushing pills into his anus. Then there was Ann. Fifty-something, plump and whose interest in life only reawakened when the tea and cakes trolley rattled through the door.

Phil, also, was unemployed and I convinced my boss to hire him as a reprographics assistant, replacing his predecessor, a girl from Skelmersdale who had simply vanished from the face of the Earth during a lunch break. Nobody seemed to care that she might have been abducted; she's probably on Zeta

Reticuli now.

It was a short-lived position, as Phil held an even weaker grasp on office politesse than me. He suffered with periodic headaches and after being stationed by a clanking photocopier for the length of a morning, he returned to his desk in a foul mood. The boss called over to him.

'Why don't you just go home if you don't want to work?'

Phil strode over, looked him square in the eye and said, 'Why don't *you* go and do some underwater farts?'

The remnants of a half-finished, Mr Kipling creamed bun still lodged in her mouth, Ann let out a superbly Dickensian 'Oooooooooohhhh!' that rose in scale as the eyes widened in grotesque disbelief.

Fin.

Back to Mrs Minkin.

We continued to write some new songs, some of which were co-written with Peter Thomas who was, in truth, primarily a guitarist rather than a bass player. Where Phil once idolised Pete Townshend, Thomas looked to Keith Richard. The sound began to change, becoming heavier, which was a direction that I wanted Raymonde to head in.

The idea was that Raymonde would expand to incorporate two guitarists and a new bass player. In my opinion, it was a creative transition and a necessary one if Raymonde was to breathe new life and reinvent itself.

We began to experiment with imagery and made a short colour film on Super 8mm for the purpose of using it in the background of live performances. Amateurishly Warholian and with no narrative, it was a collage of the group members in drag.

Peter was dressed in a polka dot skirt, white ankle socks and an Alice band, evincing the image of a superannuated schoolgirl who might stab you in the eye with a pencil. Simon, who put tremendous effort into it, came out as Eleanor Bron. Phil looked like Phil, but in a frock. I wore the lingerie of a Forty Second Street hooker. Well, not literally. Some of these images are on the front sleeve of the last Raymonde single, 'Destination: Breakdown'.

As sensitive and tactful as Peter might have been, Phil perceived the presence of another guitarist in the group to be a challenge to his position and artistic authority. I understood this and went to lengths to mollify him, assuring him that nobody was trying to usurp his position. But it was to no avail.

Ultimately, his personality makeup could not accept the inclusion of Peter into the songwriting team and, after three never less than eventful years, he left Raymonde.

I cried.

Fate took a turn in Raff Edmunds who managed The Buzzcocks and worked as chief A & R at the independent label Immaculate Records. They were also a distribution centre with a warehouse beneath its offices. This was convenient because, after the termination of a meeting, I could wander down there and loot the aisles to my heart's content.

Edmunds was a good deal older than us, then in his fifties, and had survived decades of psychedelia. He was tall with a shock of black hair and a face cleft from a Bram Stoker novel. Highly gesticulatory, he was very excited at the prospect that Acid-inspired music was making a comeback.

We brokered a one-off single deal with Immaculate Records

which allowed us to release the new Raymonde single, 'Destination: Breakdown'. I was determined to stick a colon into a song title; why should The Marvelettes have all the fun? Also, we made our first promotional video. I was delirious at seeing myself on screen for the very first time.

The video, purely performance based, was made for a small sum, most of which was allocated to the design of a Raymonde backdrop, by two film students whose names I cannot now recall. We named them Pagett Pictures in homage to the British actress Nicola Pagett.

I wore a black suit with a fake-fur hat: the look I was aiming for was "Jackie Onassis on The Bowery". Peter Thomas and our new bassist, Mark "Chicken" Sanderson wore leather. Simon Hoare sat behind the drum kit in the kind of cheap leopard-print coat and patent knee boots that would have interested the Yorkshire Ripper; looking as he did like the missing mugshot in Peter Sutcliffe's gallery of the fallen.

The reviews for 'Destination: Breakdown', if one takes notice of such things, were probably the best we had ever received. The B-side of the single was a track written and recorded in the studio in a matter of hours, titled 'Dyke on a Bum Trip'. That was our swansong. Without Phil, it simply wasn't, and couldn't be, Raymonde. And so, we quietly disbanded in early 1989 as another group rose from its ashes.

Twenty years have passed since then, but I have an affection for Raymonde that has grown rather than diminished with time. I don't habitually listen to my own records but I played *Babelogue* recently.

Lyrics are like diaries that offer up the canvas of past feelings, situations and the people who have populated one's life. If my past were a place, it is a secluded alleyway littered with the bodies of ex-bass players.

One should guard against sentimentality because it can be dangerous and unfaithful. But I imagine the affection I feel is bound up with the fondness of my youth and its frivolous indulgences. The 1980s is several lifetimes ago.

Nowadays, of course, we know that youth may last at least well into one's forties. Some of us may stretch the elastic of juvenescence into our fifties.

And why not?

However, there comes a point when one should toddle off the stage, otherwise there is the risk of appearing like an embalmed contestant at an underage beauty pageant. One should know when to let go. But they weren't going to get rid of me that easily. And a new adventure lay ahead.

RPLA:
THE LIPSTICK SWINDLE

AT THE PHOTO SESSION THE AIR was so fertile with testosterone that anybody was in danger of getting pregnant. The photographer himself, whose name thankfully escapes me, reacted to the occasional exhaust of his own flatulence as if ravished by original wit.

I knew, from the outset, that it was going to be a difficult road.

Simon Hoare (drums, castanets, red PVC), Peter Kinski (guitar) and myself were somewhat versed in the ways of business after our experience with Raymonde. When in the corporate boardroom, the primary edict is: if you can't look like Joan Crawford, then at least behave like Joan Crawford. Admit nothing and claim everything. Equipped with John Kennedy, one of the smartest lawyers in the industry, RPLA negotiated a five album deal with EMI Records which, potentially, committed them to a significant investment subsequent to those options being taken.

Rock was in the ascendant in the 1990s. Our brand of rock and roll, equal measures of The Cult, the New York Dolls and the Shangri La's, was not devastatingly original but it was loud, road-tested and could be grasped by anyone since Jim Marshall built one of those cabinet thingies with twiddly knobs that roadies like to carry and plug into the National Grid.

I had coaxed my very long hair into a Lifetime Achievement Award from Vidal Sassoon. We understood the classical essence of leather and drenched ourselves in it. Importantly, I was ready to inject some ambiguity into the game.

There was a honeymoon period in which we were fêted: garlands, Belgian chocolate, Big Car Both Ways. To EMI, we represented a proposition of breaking the American market, and there was a tremendous expectation that RPLA would swiftly progress to box-office prosperity.

They visualised us as a kind of low-cal, long distance, sinewy type animal; a jaguar, if you like, in contrast to Axel Rose's octave-breaking, bellied bluster as Lenny the Lion who, at this stage, was already afrost with split ends and rapidly tiring.

All the elements were arguably there but for one, small fly in the Clarins: 'the' lead singer was not, shall we say, *entirely* heterosexual?

Our recently acquired New York-based manager, Peter Rudge, was a Cambridge graduate who had tour managed the Rolling Stones and whom, *allegedly*, had sent Lynyrd Skynyrd up into the skies on a half-empty tank through a flair for unbridled impatience. Personally, I believe it to be rock myth.

His negotiating style was a disarming mixture of pit bull tenacity coupled with halting charm. He was under pressure from the record company to send us out on yet another long tour of British beer palaces but, frankly, having envisaged support touring under the canopy of a more established and prestigious headliner, we found the prospect quite resistible.

I'm a fine wines and international nibbles kind of person who sees no nobility in scuffing one's pumps on the cider and amphetamine circuit. Besides, I'd imagined RPLA as moving more along the lines of a fully upholstered shortcut. This is not because I don't think that one should earn it, but I felt that I already had.

Bill Price had produced that cornerstone of acid spleen, the Sex Pistols' undeniably influential *Never Mind the Bollocks*, and was currently working on Guns N'Roses *Use Your Illusion* project. We wanted him to produce our debut album. Talks were initiated and demos were dispatched to him. Does he like it, and could he possibly fit us in?

'Yes, of course, my lovelies, do come over.'

Apparently, Axl Rose and Slash had had a dreadful falling out over a Coronation dinner service and provided we flew directly to Los Angeles—a proposal that brooked no resistance in me— we could record our opus during their absence from the Skip Saylor Studios.

Los Angeles, like Bermondsey, is one huge departure lounge filled with human cargo waiting for their gate number to clack into confirmation on the electronic roster. I had been there once before in 1987, staying at Le Parc Hotel. The air conditioning pumps the aroma of melon into its rooms; I still can't cut one without having flashbacks. The bed was an acre of the finest Egyptian cotton and it was almost impossible to leave its sumptuousness.

The American thrash metal group, Anthrax, practically lived at the hotel and were often around the rooftop swimming pool. I think it was their singer, Joey Belladonna, who came over and asked to borrow my sun screen lotion.

'No.'

'Uh?'
'*No.*'

EMI installed us at a house on Java Drive in Beverly Hills. Warren Beatty lived in the house opposite and Madonna regularly cantered past our hillside garden. The scene of the Sharon Tate murders by the Manson family adjoined our property by vertical aspect, and one could see it clearly over the iced rim of a Cosmopolitan cocktail.

The idea of Hollywood is Laurel Canyon: a jag with a blue steering wheel, a bedside telephone with a low burr, a Neiman Marcus credit account and the Douglas Sirk reverie of one's own Kirk Douglas with proper and visible arse muscles. The reality can be vastly different.

It was a soporific, dreamlike, detached experience that disinclines one to meet anybody. Meeting other people in Los Angeles is potentially fatal, in any case, and not always to be recommended. The moment you leave the house, you are forced to digest the unabridged resumé of yet another sunny optimist and would-be director from Ontario.

I like America and have traversed it many times, but occasionally one wishes to hand over a garment for dry cleaning without being held captive to an action thriller plot summary in which the female lead slips into a Möbius strip before re-emerging with a different hair tone in Act III:

'Then there's like a big explosion? Bodies everywhere. Picture *Die Hard* 2 meets *Hamlet*, but with a heart. So, anyway...'

'Yes, I think I understand. Now, about this red wine stain.'

Only a week into our sojourn and my Jackie Collins fixation had reached critical mass. Simon and I explored the shopping possibilities of Melrose, it being to our eyes one vast repository of fancy retailing.

And Peter? The smog does not agree with everyone. The expansive, sodium wilderness of LA transformed him into a plush pad hermit. He moved from bedroom to recording booth to bedroom. His disavowal of a social life was borne of a singular, determined mission to make the RPLA album with no distractions. On one occasion we tried to entice him from his cocoon with the pleasures of an amiable Cherokee call girl, but to no avail.

The call came. Bill Price received us at the studio, a whisker from the badlands of Compton, in monogrammed carpet slippers, and ushered us into a setting that might have accommodated Dame Edith Evans. This ain't rock and roll, this is a repertory theatre production of an E. F. Benson story.

It was a twilight zone of boiled sweets, handwoven rugs and sensible hours. It was staffed by a compliant assistant who, at regular intervals, served tea. That is to say, he served a tray comprising a jug of hot water, a hillock of Lipton tea bags, milk, sugar and china. Tragically, he hadn't the faintest idea of how the whole ensemble came together.

Why Americans should imagine that the British fetishise tea, as if we all live in *The Flame Trees of Thika*, is beyond me. The truth is that we dump a bag in a cup, stab it with a spoon until the water is brown, spill a drop of milk in it and stir.

The album completed and christened, *Metal Queen Hijack*, we flew back to the anticipation of EMI. They decided to suspend its release until we had attracted a "broader, grassroots fan base." In my case, this is no different to asking a paraplegic to do the

Charleston all the way up the north face of Everest. I've never quite known what that term means. However, the "roots" part I could definitely empathise with – mine certainly needed doing.

The *Miss Demeanour* tour would take in thirty assorted abattoirs countrywide, culminating at Reading's After Dark Club, a venue that was reputedly run by, and popular with, Hell's Angels. It transpired to be the best night of the tour: sexy, armed and dangerous. It was also the first time I'd experienced the freedom of a halterneck top.

After the concert, a drunk Hell's Angels was banging on the door of the dressing room. I was brushing my hair and interrogating my home answering machine.

'You know what he wants, don't you?' said Peter, panic-stricken and sizing up the small ventilation window that led out onto the car park.

'I know exactly what he wants. And he will get it shortly.'

RPLA had to be seen to be paying their dues. "Dues" is an antiquated rock and roll idea that requires that you submit yourself to squalor and degradation until "they" decide that you're worthy of a dressing room that isn't also a public toilet.

It's fine when you're twenty, but at thirty I was already beyond beer crate optimism and listening to disenchanted roadies, pouring forth their stories over late night drinking sessions. We called it "Roadies' Tears". There simply wasn't time for that. EMI, who wanted high results very quickly, were standing in the wings with an end of tax year twitch.

However, they would not give us the platform, or the promotion if you will, through which to achieve it. The truth is, we should have remained in California; that is where RPLA belonged. Certainly, I made more sense on Santa Monica Boulevard than on the Balls Pond Road.

Clamped in the jaws of ill-advertised mediocrity we were frustrated and, fatally, bored. Additionally, our assigned road crew were becoming suspicious and distant. During our customary après-gig drinks, Simon, blind on Gordon's Gin and turning decidedly coquettish, playfully propositioned members of our ale-supping, wire-thumping entourage. They didn't like it and instantly retreated, in pairs.

Morale blocked in the U-bend, Peter Kinski and our hired bassist having evaporated into a world of Nintendo and Weetabix, I became more and more austerely ladylike as Simon became combative, on a tour bus irrevocably divided by mutual derision. But, at least somebody was living up to the tour name and wringing the dish towel for all it was worth.

We capitulated to the pointlessness of the campaign whilst docking at Belfast. That is not a sentence that one undertakes lightly. I remarked to an emerald about the gills Peter Rudge, who had brought us here and was now bitterly resentful of having to share the experience, how what I once felt to be liberating had now become stifling.

Rock and roll really *is* about girls and cars and little else. The crushing machismo, the misogyny and the unreconstructed ethos that I had attempted to pierce was, in fact, its very DNA. I knew full well it was going to be tough from the beginning, but I was genuinely surprised at the vigour with which these, to my mind, anachronous elements still coursed through its veins.

But this was not, I had to finally accept, the Manhattan of 1973, nor David Bowie's London of the same year, and we had, in fact, gone backwards.

Bisexuality is digestible because women are still very much in the picture. But I would rather don drag as protest than acquiesce to a confederacy of dyed in the bouffant bigots who have no sense of the real meaning of rock and roll.

Rock and roll is the inalienable right to be whoever you want to be. And if nobody else likes it, it is also the freedom to say, 'Fuck you.' Though, admittedly, this does mean a slightly reduced sales forecast.

'There's money in drag,' laughed Rudge uneasily, as we sidled into Belfast Docks.

'Yes, but I dare say you're a little old for it now, dear.'

In the earlier days of RPLA, when we were writing songs and demoing them at the "Slug Palace" in East Finchley, the house Simon and Peter shared with a motley collection of students. I met Michelle Olley, who later authored several books on erotic photography. In addition to being kept awake on the other side of a partition while the track 'Vagabond Sister' was being built from the bass drums upwards, she was a writer, editor and club organiser for the rubber fetishist magazine *Skin Two*.

I was standing in the hallway by the communal telephone, smoking, when a humanities student galloped down the stairs.

'You can't use that. I'm waiting for a transatlantic telephone call.'

Moments later, Michelle appeared and explained that the magazine was holding a Rubber Ball at the Rosemary Branch pub, and were looking for a band to play at the event. The evening was to be filmed for general video release. Getting into the spirit of things, the group wore rubber and I wore a simple but classic black, cocktail dress.

This video was passed, courtesy of our first manager and Rudge's predecessor Luxi, an idiosyncratic Bavarian related to King Ludwig, to Ron Wood of the Rolling Stones. It was later viewed on the Rolling Stones tour bus by Keith Richards and Bill Wyman. Someone suggested that we support them on the next leg of the tour, replacing the rock band Gun, who were at the point of pulling out due to illness. Allegedly, Mick Jagger took one look at the video and said: 'I'm not having her on this tour.'

What would Sigourney Weaver do given our predicament? She'd get a haircut and negotiate a sequel.

'The title of the album is *Metal Queen Hijack*. Here are the singles and this is our plan.'

By the conclusion of that meeting, which I addressed to the EMI heads standing atop the conference table in fuck-me-pumps and an Agnés B suit (a reservoir drag that predated Tarantino), the EMI mafiosi were basted in both fear and alarm. Their strategy had stalled and the till was short.

It could be said that we were trying to convince them of a more truthful and exciting agenda. Leather was out. Organza and Chanel 89 lipstick were in.

The singles were our triumvirate of queens: 'Metal Queen Hijack', 'Last Night a Drag Queen Saved Your Life' and 'The Absolute Queen of Pop'.

In the making of the three videos, the visual theme was stark minimalism, monochromatically shot and seared with crimson, to be directed by the photographer Peter Ashworth.

The vignette of the eponymous Metal Queen Hijack video single was a violent confrontation between an extraneous, gun-wielding metal queen and a symbolically homophobic metal fan sporting a vest which bore the legend: AIDS KILLS FAGGOTS.

A crude depiction perhaps, but one we felt to be axiomatic. The metal fan is summarily despatched by a bullet to the groin; penetrated anally with a high heel, and "liberated". That is what rock and roll needed: a high heel shoe up its anus. Thus, he is transmogrified into a sylphic, peacock feathered swain.

There was a duality in this message: EVOLVE OR PERISH. This was our personal ultimatum to rock and roll.

The new singles performed better than the previously released 'Unnatural Woman' and 'City of Angels', whose initial title was 'Satanic' and which, regrettably, I changed under the force of an aggressive EMI directive. However, there existed a vigilance on the part of the mainstream music press to ignore us. They had smelt the perfume. Together with a now "betrayed" rock music press, a *fatwa* was issued.

Every band that I have ever felt any passion for has, at some point, been lined up against a wall and assassinated by a journalistic firing squad. To me, this is always a good sign. We might asphyxiate on the monoxide of negative reviews, but we remained insouciant. Feeling not unlike aliens in a hostile environment, the air out there was deadly but invigorating.

'And of course we'll have to play down this whole queer thing.'

These words were uttered to me by an American A & R director looking for evidence that I might once have had a girlfriend—either living or deceased—and wearing a shirt spun of pure malicious sentiment that later insinuated itself into my dreams.

'We don't need Nebraska, Mr Shulman, we have Sybil Roscoe', I responded.

They were undecided whether to risk our ambiguity with an American public, which is an insult to American audiences. We were ambivalent. In light of the aforementioned press lockdown, we had engaged a PR team. We booked ourselves into preferred venues and were now, at least, enjoying ourselves. The radio broadcasters Ned Sherrin and the DJ Tommy Vance had sent us RSVPs for appearances on national radio.

The 'Metal Queen Hijack' video was creating a modest impact in music clubs nationwide and club proprietors had been invited to file small report cards to EMI on behalf of their clientele:

[Example]

'I came out for a drink with my mates. Who wants to see cocks being blown up?' Militant lesbians do.

Significantly, the video had also made the roster at MTV and we were a news item under the headline: "GAY ROCK?"

Why the question mark? Polysexual rock might have been more appropriate: we were gay, bisexual, heterosexual, and one of us had unnatural feelings towards Princess Anne. But there was little point in splitting proclivities now. In fact, why not liberally sow exotica into the common garden of England?

[Excerpt from a BBC Radio 1 interview]

'I was only nineteen when I appeared in *I Sailed to Tahiti with an All Boy Crew*. I'd hate that to get out now, it could really harm my image.'

It was pure fabrication designed to attract more column inches and to cause a frisson in a pop landscape which, in its tedium, thought wearing a little black eyeliner was the height of teen excitement.

To put the record straight:

I.

HAVE.

NEVER.

APPEARED.

IN.

A.

PORNO.

MOVIE.

If I had, I would have hoped for one with a more convincing title. I might have graduated to master class embroidery in the desire to oil the wheels of publicity had I not been reminded that my family were, at that moment, attentively sitting around the tea table, listening.

Locomotion, at last. By the summer of 1993, RPLA were billed to play at the Gay and Lesbian Pride festival in London, where we were interviewed and filmed by Channel Four for an upcoming mini-documentary.

At the time, Colin Ireland, the British serial killer, was yet to be captured and was already several bodies into his nocuous career. On stage we were introduced by that antipodean trage-dienne and whisky fiend Val Lehman, otherwise known as Bea Smith, bigwig and Chief Hoffman presser in the television programme *Prisoner Cell Block H*.

Admittedly, flushed with a little something, I began to wave a large and very real gun about in advocacy of defence against hate crimes. Like an escapee from a William Burroughs' novel, I called for everybody to arm themselves and obtain false passports

After the set, I swanned off stage and immediately walked into the fairy godmother grandee of Stonewall, otherwise known as Sir Ian McKellen. He shot me a look of majestic, Shakespearean dudgeon. His eyes bore directly into mine with impressive disesteem and admonishment. Well, if anyone can do it, he can. My answer was schoolgirlish: 'I don't care. I'm *glad*.'

EMI, meanwhile, were conspicuous by their absence. Our manager, Peter Rudge, had become a phantom condemned, it seemed, to forever remain at lunch. It was an arrangement that suited us perfectly since his particular talents were now superfluous to us.

'The Absolute Queen of Pop' had garnered good reviews. Eventually, given the green light to release our album, we booked the Milch Gallery in London for its launch. The event was also filmed for Carlton Television's *The Big E* programme featuring an interview with Morrissey by two of its presenters, the Cleavage Sisters.

By this time, we had collected a retinue of drag queens who would invade a stage already precipitously groaning under the weight of all that gold lamé. Potential collapse of the stage was an ever present highlight of our performances. Many people were there that night, including Sigue Sigue Sputnik—another proponent of the court shoe—and Gilbert and George. It might have been a fabulous, one-night Hoxton extravaganza but it was also too late.

Our account with EMI Records was in debit; our supporters in that company had moved on to new pastures and we held all the allure of an immaculately turned out liability. I was also in debt. After receiving the sober news from my long-suffering accountant, Gerald, that the UK Inland Revenue had lodged a £20,000 tax claim against me, I went directly to an upscale travel agency. To me, all tax is theft. I booked a round the world holiday with a carpetbag of Hilton hotel vouchers, taking in the spas of World Heritage sites: Sydney, Rio de Janeiro, Paris and Cairo. It was the last splurge.

EMI finally released the album through contractual obligation rather than in the spirit of restored faith. Furthermore, they sanctioned no plan to promote it. A rather good rock album was interred, without ceremony, and RPLA were to be hushed up. They were resolute. Perceiving themselves to be victim of a Machiavellian deceit, we were released from the label. The masquerade was over, as Timi Yuro once sang.

The aforementioned documentary commissioned by Channel Four for the programme *Naked City* was broadcast in the autumn of 1993. It briefly explored the question of whether the rock and roll genre could ever clasp an openly gay rock group to its Iron Maiden breast plate; specifically alighting on the controversy surrounding RPLA's metamorphosis from apparent orthodoxy to lipstick nihilism. The writer and author Jon Savage, a Queer Music historian and self-appointed Professor of Punk, concluded with these comments:

'Pop music is one of the only places in society where people can talk about homosexuality. If they're not talking about it, they're denying it, which is what happened in the mid-1980s in Heavy Metal and why everybody made homophobic statements.

They couldn't cope with the reality of playing very hard rock dressed in girly clothes. There is a truism that if you declare yourself to be gay your record sales will fall. I think the attitude is: you don't know until you try.'

Well, I did. And they do.

RPLA was also included in another television programme satirising the excesses of rock and roll titled *Rock' n' Roll Babylon*, featuring Iggy Pop, Keith Moon and Aerosmith.

Our last performance took place on a flatbed truck in Times Square, New York City for the filming of a video to support the American release of 'The Absolute Queen of Pop' through the Collision Arts/Warner label.

We were staying at the Chelsea Hotel, which is the real Rock and Roll Hall of Fame. Somebody was shot on the first floor, literally minutes after check-in, and I discovered that the Beat writer Herbert Huncke was lodging in the room next to mine. I had read *And The Evening Sun Turned Crimson* and wondered how I might devise an introduction. A New York friend of mine offered to knock on his door and smooth the way. She returned shortly and said, 'He wants money.'

'I don't have any cash. Will he accept a Bradford & Bingley cheque supported by a cheque card?'

Times Square. It was a warm, spring evening and the theatres emptied their audiences onto Broadway. For me it was the realisation of an adolescent dream: to sing my *saeta* to the commuters of the Bronx, Brooklyn and Queens, engulfed by the Rechy-esque, kaleidoscopic neon of the Great White Way. The next day we were returning home, officially unemployed.

Yet what should have been the nadir was, ultimately, sublime.

HAIRCENTRICITY

FOR SOME, HAIR IS the first thing we notice in someone. One's eye is immediately drawn to the top of the head before we assess other, necessarily more vital features such as eyes, mouth or even ears. We discern the hairstyle before we learn that a person has only one eye or perhaps a cleft palate. In strangers—and strangers potentially become acquaintances, friends and even lodgers—the hair is surveyed and it is sometimes on this basis that we decide whether to risk a beverage or, less importantly, full penetration with its owner.

I say less importantly because coffee is more dangerous than heroin: it leads to conversation, careless asides and confession. Whereas you can engage in penetration with someone without admitting to your full birth name or true shoe size. Far less risky.

My hair has had a varied and, dare I say, adventurous life. I began life as a child in the early 1960s. In that decade, we put a man on the Moon, The Beatles dominated half the hemisphere and the civil rights movement blazed across our television screens. Although, for me, this decade is more notable for the fact that all bridesmaids were forced into lemon, regardless of their complexion. It was a socially conservative era when men had very little dominion over their hairstyles, yet had the freedom to jump on and off Routemaster buses at will, molest female strangers in public, and smoke cigarettes whilst playing sports.

I was locked into a crew cut, shorn regularly by a monthly pantomime at a Sicilian barber shop in East Street, Walworth. After what must have been a considerable time in England, his vocabulary still mainly consisted of pointing. My mother would point to a picture on the wall of a young man with an army crew cut, and he would point at my head and say, '*Si-mi-lair.*'

'Yes, similar.'

This association endured for years; for my part exclusively seated, for his stood on a small orange crate behind me as he gradually shrunk in stature over the years.

The 1970s was an exciting time in many respects, and I think it can be said that, as the new idea of unisex salons sprang up on every available corner, never has a decade spawned such a rich variety of hairstyles.

Almost everybody carried a comb or a brush and the introduction of the pocket-sized hairspray canister meant that one could "touch up" in full view of a heaving, Saturday afternoon high street. Similarly, as the 1960s heralded the Age of Aquarius, the 1980s was the Age of Haircentricity.

My hair grows rather quickly, and most of my teenage years were spent trying to grow my hair to a shoulder length, measuring its progress in the mirror with a ruler in my hand. I had, in fact, only four inches to go before it reached its target destination: David Johansen on the reverse sleeve of the New York Dolls' debut album. It was forcibly cut because my school exercised a hair length policy. I lost months. You can't imagine the tears. It was like trying to compose a song lyric while a sentry with an eraser dutifully rubbed out the first stanza. And they wonder why I became so malicious.

I eventually gave up this ambition and, for many years, wore my hair in the style of James Dean, which suited my apparel of jeans, boots, t-shirt and windcheater. By the mid-1980s my quiff, which now added a crucial four inches to my height, reached its zenith.

The amount of hair lacquer required to keep a quiff erect in the event of a strong gale—or a Force 9 on the Beaufort scale (larger branches break off trees, damage to circus tents and canopies)—veered towards industrial quantities. I'm surprised that I didn't suffer with chemical poisoning to the scalp. What does not surprise me is that there is a James Maker-sized hole in the ozone layer.

A note on quiffs: you can wear it high while young but one should keep it short as the years advance, otherwise one may look like a persecuted homosexual solicitor in a Dirk Bogarde vehicle. Although, granted, there are worse things to look like.

Colour-wise, I have run the gamut from peroxide blonde to ash blonde, light chestnut, auburn, dark brown and finally black.

The ash blonde period was interesting but brief. I saw the actor Richard Bradford in the series *Man in A Suitcase* and thought that this shade, which is almost silver, would look quite striking on a twenty-five-year-old. So, I had my hair professionally dyed before a holiday to Tunisia. However, I was forced to remain, for the duration of the trip, within the hotel grounds to avoid sexual harassment by excited cheroot vendors.

In any case, adjusting one's hair colour to the opposite end of the spectrum necessitates constant vigilance and one's hairdresser becomes an indispensable and costly guardian.

Auburn, I believe, was an accident caused by a chemical reaction in the DNA of my hair that introduced a surfeit of red into the colour scheme, lending me the appearance of Sarah Miles in *Ryan's Daughter*. It took an absolute age to grow out because dyeing on top of red is like trying to give Anne Frank a happy ending.

Apart from a light trim, I did not cut my hair from 1988 through to 1992. In those five years, it grew to a length only a hand's width from my waist. These were the "Rita Hayworth years" when the longer my hair grew, the more impossible I became to deal with; the more forthright my pronouncements on both domestic and international affairs; and the longer my stretches sat in the airing cupboard in a head towel conditioning my hair with virgin olive oil.

I decided to give myself a face lift in the form of a corkscrew perm, which took inches from its length but produced a volume so bounteous that I abandoned public transport altogether, and could travel only by saloon car. There is a photograph of my hair seen through the back window of a Mercedes leaving a fashionable West End discotheque, but sadly it is now lost and cannot be included in this book.

The maintenance of my hair now occupied about 30% of my waking hours, added to which I had begun to experiment with a beard. The beard was quickly renounced: facial hair does not suit me, it makes me look like an unreliable Balkan plumber.

One afternoon the decision was made, on my behalf, to visit

an old-style barber, and to relieve everybody of what had clearly become a bête-noire. The relief was immediate, notwithstanding the fact that I had now gained an extra three hours in the day. Also, my hairdryer was seized. A small, white van arrived for its collection and it was later destroyed in a controlled explosion, behind a Plexiglass screen.

Since, I have again returned to the crew-cut and my hair is now liberally flecked with grey.

I do not believe that men should dye their hair after the age of forty. Many men do, and often in black which, rather than restoring youth and virility, instead makes one look haunted; the eyes recede further into their sockets, the harsh colour giving one a mortuary table *come hither* look. I sat through such a transformation at my local hairdresser's, and an attractive sixty-year-old man rose from the chair looking like Davros (King of the Daleks) in a wig.

But one thing is certain: if one goes bald, shave it off, because when the parting moves inexorably from the top of the head to just above the ear, nature is nudging you towards the semblance of an unreliable Persian cabaret entertainer.

Which, of course, many of us are.

THE CUMBERLAND SAUSAGES
ARE MINE

My first scene entailed running down a long, steep flight of unforgiving, stone steps attached to a piece of sixteenth century fortification. I was to bound down them, landing at a marked spot, before striding over to another character to speak my first lines with a highly arched left eyebrow — my trademark.

Literally, I picked my way down those steps, the body turned sideways, the face a mask of gingerly intent and the tongue extruding between the lips in fierce concentration. Handrails had not been invented in the sixteenth century, and to the left of me was an appreciable drop to the cacti-studded massif that the castle stood on.

In effect, my premature vertigo had doubled the time length of the scene. This is rather clever if you can convince the director to keep it. However, rather than the envisaged shot of a noble lord's dramatic entrance, it instead offered up a television commercial for the sale of a home-fitted stairlift.

It was my opening debut in a major motion picture and one that many an unestablished actor would covet - and I couldn't cope with the stairs. In my defence, I'd like to say that the tread-depth of antique Spanish steps were designed for antique Spanish people. I know this because I have been living with them for several years. I was wearing a pair of size 9 thigh boots and was also carrying a heavy sword.

Marcus Thompson, the director, beckoned me over to the shade of an oleander tree.

'I think we need to put a bit more sex into the stair scene. Try and have some fun with it?' he suggested, ceaselessly tucking his hair behind his left ear.

'Yes, I see. Let's do another take,' I said.

I went up the stairs again and came back down in exactly the same manner as before, only this time I completed only half the descent before someone mercifully shouted, 'Cut!' The production manager motioned me over to the bottom of the steps.

'Look, ducky, all you've got to do is fly down them, hit your mark and start your dialogue. Just fly down them!'

'And kill myself. It's okay for you, *ducky*, you're in trainers. If somebody had forewarned me I could have practised at home, I live in a high rise.'

I stomped back up to the top. By this time the rest of the cast and crew members had ambled over to see what all the fuss was about, providing me with an audience to magnify the humiliation.

'Rollover. And Action!'

My third descent went well until an inquisitive hornet began to buzz me, and from the confines of my wig I could see that it had lodged itself in a curl within millimetres of my eye. I lost my nerve, wrenched the wig off, tossed it over the parapet, and ran back up to where I'd started. The production manager doggedly climbed up to meet me.

'What's your fucking problem with these stairs? They're just stairs.'

'But that's like saying to Anne Frank "Oh, come on, World War Two wasn't *that* bad". I want to see Marcus.'

Finally, they decided to film my head at the top of the steps, but my feet from the fifth step from the bottom, allowing me to descend without impaling myself on my sword.

Middleton's Changeling was a screen adaptation of the Jacobean bloodfest *The Changeling* written in 1622 by Thomas Middleton and William Rowley. I met Marcus Thompson in 1990 when RPLA chose him to direct the video of our debut single, 'Unnatural Woman'. A filmmaker and painter, he was given to occasional gregariousness and knew everything about *mise en scene* yet was unable to butter toast.

When I first met him, he was then married to his first wife, Judy, a filmmaker, author and artist with whom I remain good friends to this day. She managed him, in every sense of the word. During those storyboard meetings at the EMI Records offices in Manchester Square, an assistant would enter the boardroom bearing his daily allowance: a packet of Silk Cut, a Caramac and two one pound coins, all carefully sellotaped together.

After the completion of the 'Unnatural Woman' video, filmed on a vast stage at Pinewood Studios and featuring a set of one thousand candles that had to be painstakingly snuffed and relit between takes, I began to visit Marcus and Judy at their home in deepest Surrey. An association and a friendship formed respectively, and one evening I was given the film script for *Middleton's Changeling*, to play the part of Tomazo de Piracquo.

Piracquo is the brother of Alonzo who is betrothed to

Beatrice. However, before the marriage Beatrice falls in love with Alsemero and plots, aided by her manservant De Flores (played by Ian Dury), to murder Alonzo.

The story of the making of this film is possibly more interesting than the film itself. Several times funding was secured, then withdrawn. The original score of Jimi Hendrix was approved by the foundation that caretook his estate, and later invalidated. Personal allegiances were lost, a divorce was instigated and a marriage was made.

It was filmed on location in Alicante, specifically at the castle of Santa Bárbara, and also on the back lot of Pinewood studios in Buckinghamshire, England. Many of the cast were relative unknowns including the leading lady, save for Billy Connolly, Ian Dury, Moya Brady who had appeared in Mike Leigh's *Life Is Sweet* and Campbell Morrison, perhaps best remembered as the Scottish, alcoholic father in the short-lived BBC soap *Eldorado*. The Mancunian poet John Cooper-Clarke and the musician and English eccentric, Vivian Stanshall, also made cameo appearances.

There were no rehearsals prior to production, and when I was driven onto the set under a broiling June sun to film my first scene, it was not without apprehension. All actors need to rehearse in order to hone their lines and to develop the chemistry of their character with the other players. Otherwise there is the danger of marching into scenes, delivering lines and slamming metaphysical doors on exit.

Providentially, I had bought my own costume in London. I knew full well that by the time I arrived in Spain the Wardrobe Department would already have been looted of its bounty, leaving me with Phyllis Calvert's old hairpiece and a pair of baggy ankle boots appropriated from *The Onedin Line.*

Later that evening, I was billeted to a remote villa on the outskirts of the city. The logistics of putting one person in a four bedroom villa while others virtually had to top and tail in cramped beach apartments eludes me. A production assistant dropped me off at the gates and sped off in a cloud of dust with a promise to collect me two days hence.

It was now nightfall. The sound of the Spanish campo is not always the tranquilising, mesmeric buzz of the cicada mating call carried by a supple breeze that plays with one's peignoir. Often it is the unceasing, depressing call of distressed dogs chained up in the yards of empty casitas, pining for their owners. Once one dog starts to bark, every *podenco* within earshot is alerted and picks up the baton, and so it is carried through the night.

No electric. No light. I was shattered and, aided by my cigarette lighter, I found a bedroom and lay down to sleep. At some point in the night, I woke up with a raging thirst and decided to locate the kitchen to see if there might be some drinkable water. I was warned not to drink the tap water. My trusty Ronson lighter guided me towards the refrigerator and, opening it, I saw a bottle of mineral water and what looked to be a pound of sausages.

Abruptly, a disembodied, booming and rather fruity voice that sounded as if it had absconded *The Tempest* declared: 'THE CUMBERLAND. SAUSAGES. ARE *MINE*!'

I froze in shock. Instinctively, I disengaged from the salad crisper to witness the phantasm of a tall, elderly man with long, white, flaxen hair draped in a Victorian nightgown and holding a church candle.

'We are in *darkness*. You will have to find whatever light you can.'

He retreated from the kitchen, into said darkness while still facing me, receding from whence he came as if borne by silent castors.

Vivian Stanshall was variously a poet, painter, raconteur and a songwriter who achieved chart success in 1968 with the song 'I'm An Urban Spaceman', performed by his group The Bonzo Dog Doo-Dah Band. He had been staying at the villa with his amanuensis, but they left the next morning to go to Barcelona "to get 'Gaudied' up."

I, meanwhile, was on the point of hallucination with thirst and hunger. Leaving the gates of the villa, I turned right in search of some provisions. The stroll became a hike, and the hike became a crawl as the sun rose ever higher. The intensity of the southern Spanish sun is not European, it is African. After perhaps ninety minutes, the road ended at the foot of a mountain. This happens a lot in Spain; you become a rambler at your peril.

Returning, I began to wander into the road. Two cars passed me yet never stopped, despite my windmilling attempts to flag them down. I flung myself through the gates, into the swimming pool, walked underwater and reemerged at the steps of the shallow end. Back through those gates, and turned left. Less than 500 metres away was a fully stocked Spar supermarket.

I could have wept. And I did, because they were closed for the siesta.

My fellow players, discounting the actors I have already mentioned, treated me with a general suspicion, if not thinly veiled derision. Perhaps it was due to the fact that I wasn't a full-time, unemployed actor and had brought with me sufficient funds to avail myself of the local bistros.

My own opinion was that if anybody deserved an Equity Card, it was me. But, then, some of my best performances have been offstage. They relented somewhat towards the end of the shoot, inviting me to an impromptu beach party.

'No, thank you, I don't really go in for campfire sing alongs,' I said, tartly.

The Spanish wrap party, held at an open-air restaurant hard by the sea, was memorable if only for the sight of Vivian Stanshall lying on the ground in a state of high inebriation, surrounded by the broken shards of spent wine glasses and waving away all attempts to help him with that tremulous, dramaturgic voice: 'LEAVE IT! *LEAVE* IT!'

My final scene was filmed at Pinewood, acting with an off-screen mannequin swathed in brocade in place of Guy Williams, my character's brother Alonzo, as he had emigrated to Kenya to run a safari park.

My partner, Paul, agreed to return John Cooper-Clarke, who was to rapid-fire one of his poems in the setting of a mental asylum, to his home in Chelmsford. It was a pleasure to spend a few hours in his company, reminiscing over the Manchester of the post-punk years.

He knew Nico when she was living in Brixton in the early 1980s and recounted some amusing anecdotes of their time together at Heroin Mansions. What their conversation might have sounded like can only be imagined: her sonorous and Teutonic euphonium of a voice that could stretch the fabric of time with a syllable, and his flat, nasal burr that beat to a Salford slate cadence. In summing up, he said:

'She were alright, were Nico. But a bit of a daft bat. Could get right on yer fookin' nerves.'

Middleton's Changeling opened in London's Leicester Square, and then vanished.

THE JEFFREY DAHMER
PARTY YEARS

RECLINING ON A BED wearing gold leather jeans, a waist length wig, smoking a cigarette and engaging in some verbal ballet, I passed into unconsciousness whilst mid-sentence, sliding off the bed onto some rush matting. Concorde was descending and approaching the runway. Similarly intoxicated, or languidly absorbed in their own couture and 6AM comedown fabulousness, no one noticed anything. Until, that is, the acrid smell of burning entered the nostrils of a semi-alert, Cypriot transvestite hairdresser. My wig was aflame. It was quickly extinguished by the repeated blows of a fellow party guest's patent Italian slingback.

This image encapsulates the 1990s party years. Having reached one's thirties it was, ostensibly, the last opportunity to misbehave before boxing away the party shoes, experimenting with facial hair, assessing the pensions market and, officially, reaching maturity. Of course, it was no such thing.

They were also the Jeffrey Dahmer years. Inspired and drawn in by Brian Masters' book, *The Shrine of Jeffrey Dahmer*, I decided that I wanted to make a documentary about Dahmer, exploring the social ripple effect of the serial killer, interviewing family members, work colleagues and the families of his victims. I embarked on thorough research into the Dahmer case and, on an elementary level, I became a student of criminology and psychology.

It was a Stygian yet compulsively interesting journey that took me to Milwaukee, where I walked in Dahmer's footsteps, meeting some of the people whose paths had crossed with his, and whose lives were irrevocably changed by the experience. The Smith family, notably, were very open and supportive of my documentary idea.

As DV video had not yet been developed, which would have meant that I could have made the film myself, with a little help, I was obliged to submit the synopsis to various film production companies so as to secure a budget. After more than a year trying to raise the money, I eventually had to abandon the project. The sticking point was that it was felt there was not enough Jeffrey Dahmer in the film: in other words, the focus was not sufficiently centred on the more visceral and sensational aspect of Dahmer's crimes.

Moving swiftly on from handsaws to handbags, the late 1990s were awash in an abundance of recreational drugs and champagne, with the strict, if not enforced, proviso that one always wore costume at its fiestas. I was a peripheral character in that I tended to dip in and out as the fancy took me, rather than ticking the Seven Day Weekend option.

The scene grew up around concentric circles of people from the arts: designers Murray & Vern and House of Harlot, photographer Peter Ashworth, club doyenne Kim and a number of musicians including Robert Michael— better known as DJ

Serotina—who, sadly, is no longer with us. Simon Hoare had formed a new band called Salon Kitty with Michelle Olley as co-writer and lead singer.

Salon Kitty became a fixture on London's fetish and club scene with their electro pop music shot through with elements of John Barry and Marc Almond. Their mission, quite simply, was to have a good time, all of the time. Their early performances could at times be a little shambolic, yet it all somehow hung together because they were fun and, importantly, they were a gang. All the best groups are gangs.

Salon Kitty were signed by the major record label Epic who were intrigued by them, yet at a total visionary loss as to how to market them. Epic sat on them for a year before finally releasing them.

Simon was also manager of a reputable fetish clothing store in Holloway which doubled as a drop-in social centre that placed him at that scene's nucleus. Noko of Apollo 440, with whom I recorded and toured as James Maker & Noko 440 in 2004, and his then-partner Kristine, often threw lavish parties in the vast aircraft hangar in which they lived.

At those parties there was nearly always a crescendo; whether it be a manic depressive guest slitting his wrists in the bathroom, liberally spraying the tiles with a Jackson Pollock in rhesus negative, or the dramatic collapse of a heavy, Gothic altar onto a long banqueting table at which people were sat discussing their own gorgeousness.

It stood, unsecured, on an impressive antique sideboard that held an extensive collection of absinthe, mescal, international liqueurs and an actual stuffed monkey. Michelle had moved from a barstool directly in front of it only seconds before it groaned and crashed onto the table. It is a small miracle that she wasn't paralysed or killed. Yet, in high style, the party carried on.

At others there might be a spontaneous interlude: a lesbian floor show, a demonstration in the art of flagellation or a surrealist vignette. Simon often performed the latter with a piece titled *Trailer Park Trash*. This early morning theatre consisted of coming on to a ZZ Top record, wearing a long blond wig that covered his entire face, a pair of Ray-Ban Wayfarers and delivering a monologue on being the stud of a trailer park before stripping to stockings and panties, metamorphosing into his own daughter.

The later stage version omitted the "scrotum over the lit candle" element of the original.

It was at one of the earlier parties given in 1994 that I first took ecstasy. Unfortunately, I later took a pre-med chaser. A woman in a bespoke latex air stewardess outfit came round with a tray, circulating them. Very civilised.

Occasionally we would go to an after-hours club located within a maze of corridors under a railway arch in East London. Its proprietors and clientele were, for the most part, mature transvestites who resembled fallen women from 1950s B-movies, and along with their admirers. Although, it also attracted many a clubgoer who wouldn't, or couldn't, go home and who could squeeze past the door lady, Maureen. By way of beverages the bar offered only beer, vodka and GHB.

Gamma Hydroxybutyrate is a colourless, odourless drug that can increase the libido and removes inhibitions. It can also be fatal, both physically and socially; once I witnessed the spectacle of people pairing off to have sex, leaving a single man who, with no partner, proceeded to "fuck" a chair.

One evening, a transvestite in a severe black bobbed wig and PVC miniskirt was overcome by a mixture of alcohol and GHB, semi-collapsing whilst still technically standing, over the back of a biscuit-coloured velour couch. This was nothing particularly unusual and, therefore, anyone actually sitting on the couch would have continued whatever they were doing, perhaps exercising a little caution not to ignite said person's wig with their Rothmans.

Morals and scruples being as relevant as breasts on an avocado at this venue, a Turkish cab driver, unable to contain himself at the sight of this slumped lovely, unzipped his fly and proceeded to take advantage. She was hardly released when another cab driver followed suit. What they could not have known is that they had unwittingly committed their first act of necrophilia. On closing, all attempts by the proprietor and staff to revive her failed.

Many of us departed the scene that I speak of, which gradually imploded as it shifted from the axis of absurdity, fun and creative hem lining to an orgy of cannibalism.

Courtesy of Michelle Olley, who opened certain doors for me, I was working as an itinerant writer and columnist for various lifestyle magazines such as *Attitude*, *Fable* and *Pure*. I contrived to write a hotel review that incorporated a chance meeting in the spa with the deceased British television actress Yootha Joyce, and a review of a restaurant that I had never visited.

'The food was ecumenical in flavour. The wine was an unpretentious Pécharmant from the Périgord Noir. Quite excellent, although if it gets too much of the Dordogne wind it has a tendency to sulk. They must try harder with their pesto, which did not so much remind me of Liguria, but the Co-op.'

I was fired from one magazine for telling the editor that I was completely untouched by Barbra Streisand and, in fact, considered *Yentl* to be a crime against the cinema-going public.

We were attempting to leave London and to relocate to Los Angeles. Paul, was working as an Art Director on commercials and we were formulating the plan to emigrate. Emigration to the United States is a difficult affair unless you can satisfy the authorities that you are either rich, uniquely talented on an international basis, or a refugee from a war zone. I could have applied to the American Embassy on the latter consideration, but I instead tried the fourth way: marry a lesbian.

I found a candidate through the small ads of a paper. Kathy from Buffalo was seeking a mutually beneficial arrangement with a British male. I contacted her and we arranged to rendezvous in the shabby chic foyer and bar of the Little Bit Ritzy cinema in Brixton.

This cinema specialised in showing independent or obscure films and B-movies. On the evening that I arrived they were showing *They Saved Hitler's Brain* but whoever had climbed the ladder to the billing marquee with a bucket of giant Scrabble had announced it as *They Saved Hitler's Brian*. That, I think, would have made for a more interesting film.

On entering the foyer, I instinctively strode towards a handsome woman, bedecked in vintage denim and seated on a bar stool. I was about to greet her when I felt a tap on my right shoulder. I turned round and, looking down, saw what appeared to be a small, bird-like head with an expression of beady-eyed, insistent recognition, atop a pair of novelty leggings.

'Hi, I'm Kathy from Buffalo!' she chirped.

We ordered drinks and she ushered me over to a banquette. Admittedly, I am not *au courant* in the fashion stakes but then neither have I teamed a pair of novelty leggings with a customised t shirt that shouts: HI! LIKE 50% DON'T WANT PERSHING?

I wish I had been wearing a similar t shirt that shouted back: HI! LIKE NOVELTY LEGGINGS SHOULD BE ERADICATED, INCLUDING THE PEOPLE IN THEM?

She was overly perky in that way people essay when they are disguising manic depression; always inches away from a windowsill. Within fifteen minutes, I had learnt that she lived in a lesbian co-operative household; used several aliases, could not digest rennet and hyperventilated at the thought of crossing water. The bottom line was a proposal that I marry her that very week.

Visions surged up before my eyes of a framed wedding picture of me with a Kafkaesque hydrophobic, rescuing her from a variety of architecturally undemanding bridges (London has thirty-three to choose from), while ploughing through an Everest of forms and paperwork.

The allure of California rapidly evaporated as the realisation hit me that the true obstacle to a ranch style bungalow in Topanga Canyon was not so much the rigorous and protracted selection procedure of the U.S. immigration service. Rather, it was the fact that I am an unrepentant smoker.

I was forty. Paul was on location working on a film and was unable to return to London to spend the celebrations with me. I was determined not to pass that particular milestone sat in an armchair, benevolently smiling through an open window at children playing. So I booked a flight to Arrecife in Lanzarote, where no one knew me—for I wanted no witnesses—and ushered in The Big 40 dancing to flamenco music on a zinc-topped bar in front of a modest, yet appreciative audience oiled on *Licor 43*.

I had a wonderful time; I'm not quite so sure they did. A pattern, as you see, emerges.

At forty, and beyond, a sense of mortality begins to enter the equation. Some friends fall away, others, in fact, die prematurely. Also, the social landscape changes as a number of those in one's circle divorce. Unfortunately, one is almost always forced to take sides; it's rarely possible to be nonpartisan. Some of my male friends had left their spouses to live with a younger partner.

Of course, relationships have their timespan and people part, or fall in love, for a manifold of reasons. The older man chasing the quarry of a younger woman, or younger man, is now a situation comedy cliché. It is possible to see it as the reassertion of virility before the onset of prostate complications.

For some, youthfulness is very much a factor in the selection of a partner. It can be driven by the fear of ageing and of death but, also, naturally by passion. There is an element of vampirism in sinking your bridgework into the near-pristine throat of someone who was yet to be born while you were tuning into *Knots Landing*.

The only problem with intergenerational relationships, as I see it, is that there exists the ultimate and very real prospect of attending your lover's fortieth birthday party by virtue of a web cam set up in a hospice, wearing a silly hat that has been forced on you. Death is a messier business than birth, and I cannot contemplate a worse scenario than having my nappy changed by an underpaid Ghanaian intern, to the chilling jollity of Russ Abbot's 'Atmosphere', whilst trying to keep track of a party in Penge.

In any case, I had thus far escaped my worst fear: I had not *quite* yet thrown myself through the revolving doors of the millinery section of Selfridge's, reemerging to address everyone as "Honky Tonk".

I have seen this happen to people. From thereon in, the eyes dart from left to right in perpetual panic, the buttons popping on a shirt designed to be worn by Kate Moss, the inexorable slide of the toupee into comic value after three Tia Marias and the evening closing with the *harrumph!* of frustration as one's Plan is thwarted.

This, together with the fact that my mouth had still not turned *inoperably upside down* through a series of disappointments, was a triumph. But, certainly, it was time to take stock of one's life; to ask oneself certain questions and to weigh up the future, for it always arrives, usually when one is least prepared.

THE RUNAWAY CONSTABLE

THERE AREN'T MANY THINGS in life I regret, but I still feel a tinge of guilt about Edinburgh. It wasn't exactly my fault. I was in a state of shock. Besides, I had only agreed to come along to break the tedium of a winter West London skyline.

Paul was inside The Royal Bank of Scotland trying to find out where to deliver a priceless Constable painting, unaware that outside both it and me were hurtling towards a busy traffic intersection.

The lorry had slipped out of its parking gear and began to reverse into the road and down the hill, one of those scenic ones Edinburgh is famous for. It gathered momentum surprisingly quickly and, unable to find the brake—I wasn't wearing my contact lenses—I decided to jump ship. I ran alongside it, holding onto the passenger door handle. Perhaps I thought that I should at least be *seen* to be trying to halt this seven and one-half tonne truck. It was now travelling faster than I could run and, reluctantly, I let go of the handle and followed behind as it rapidly approached the cross street.

A bus packed with fish-eyed commuters swung into view and directly into the path of the lorry.

Commuter carnage.

Air ambulances.

Breaking News.

And me being led away in handcuffs to assist the police with their enquiries. Prison, of course, and years spent trying to avoid the affections of a big, great, hairy multiple strangler called Cuddles. I was already envisioning it:

'Come on, babes.'

'Not tonight, Cuddles.'

'Babes...'

'Not *tonight*.'

When circumstances leap beyond your control, panic subsides and a strange yet pleasant calmness envelopes you. It is not dissimilar to being the protagonist in a silent movie, but with less makeup. Time stood still, as did I. I watched as the lorry gained on the bus and through the windows I could see its occupants: two dozen mouths stretched open in Munchian elongation, mute with disbelief, in a collective: OH. MY. GOD.

The panicked driver, seeing what was headed his way, frantically accelerated, avoiding a collision with only a few feet to spare. I gave chase again as the lorry continued down the hill, waving at the commuters as I ran past, essaying a look of fleeting yet profound apology.

At the bottom of the hill was a small park surrounded by cars, and this is where the scene abruptly ended. The lorry smashed into the side of a chocolate coloured Honda Civic carrying a disabled parking badge. The passenger door was now on the wrong side of the vehicle, broken glass littered its seats and, quite clearly, it was a write-off. The lorry was unscratched, save for some chocolated coloured flakes of paint on its rear bars.

I ran back up the hill and, on reaching the Royal Bank of Scotland, I saw Paul coming out. I didn't say anything, I couldn't say anything, but instead performed a sort of mime of the events that would have done the Prague Puppet Theatre proud. He retrieved the lorry and the Constable, and instructed me to place a note on the Honda Civic owner's windscreen.

We left Scotland with haste. As we bumped over the Cheviots of Northumbria he said to me:
    'You've left the note?'
    'Yes.'
    'With all my details.'
    'Details?'
    'Driver registration number, phone number.'
    'Not exactly.'
    'What did you write?'
    '"Sorry".'

One of those commuters observed the licence plate of the lorry and, on our return to London, Paul was invited to visit the police station. Wisely, he omitted to mention me, which could only have complicated matters, and an insurance claim was lodged by the Honda Civic owner.
    I tell this story because, since then, I see Edinburgh as a calamitous metaphor for much of my life.

MR MAKER
CHANGES TRAINS

AT THE TURN OF THE NEW MILLENNIUM I was staying temporarily in the East Village, Manhattan. A friend of mine, Krisahn, had met a new boyfriend who often went to Wyoming in pursuit of his passion for winter sports. Hence, he whisked her off to Jackson Hole to teach her how to ski.

I stayed at her apartment on East 11th Street to look after her dog, which was rescued from a pound in the Bronx.

I, too, adopted a dog, a crossbreed Alsatian, from Battersea Dogs Home in the early 1980s. The affair lasted less than a week. She was too distressed and I was not mature enough to handle her vomiting, defecation, and barking constantly the moment I attempted to leave the flat. I spent five days, in white ankle socks, mopping. She had to be returned; I was not a fitting owner.

As she bundled her bags into a waiting yellow cab, I called down to her from the fire escape, a wet tea towel over my forearm.

'Call me when you get there!'

'OK.'

'Don't drink anything carbonated on the flight, you'll bloat, intestinal gases!'

'OK.'

'Keep flexing your toes, thrombosis!'

'OK.'

'And don't come back pregnant, you haven't got a prenuptial!'

'Oh, this is *awful*.'

In the following weeks, I explored Manhattan, visiting its museums, galleries and neighbourhood taverns; from Harlem in the north to the Red Hook district across the river which inspired Hubert Selby Jr. to write *Last Exit to Brooklyn*, the book that prompted me to crayon that Bermondsey road sign so many years before.

One evening I saw David Johansen and The Harry Smiths performing country blues songs in the West Village to a chicken in a basket, Bridge and Tunnel crowd. That poignant experience underscored for me how much time had passed since the salad days of unaccountability and further reminded me that, as nothing lasts forever—apart from herpes and Lulu—everything is eventually swept away. If one refuses to move, one is physically paved over.

Returning to London, Paul informed me that it was now time to enter a new phase of adult responsibility. A mortgage to buy our ex-council authority flat on the seventeenth floor of a high rise in Holland Park. Facing west, the views were impressive and offered expansive views of Shepherd's Bush, Ealing, Chiswick and further, towards Richmond and Heathrow Airport.

Holland Park is an affluent district of large, stucco villas, luxury four wheel drives and people who are skilled in the art of eating quail. At its western limit towers the 1960s utopian vision of our building. I am used to concrete, but a local residents' committee were so aggrieved at the sight of this monolith, they tried to move the borough boundary. In other words, to eject us from the Royal Borough of Kensington and Chelsea and rezone us in Hammersmith and Fulham.

It was very convenient because at the ground floor was a Costcutter supermarket. I had an account with Mr Sharma who ran it, and one could swan down in the elevator to grab a few provisions without even having to get properly dressed. Also, there was a concierge in the form of Ana, a middle-aged, mighty-elbowed West Londoner of Italian extraction who was privy to all sorts of information and gossip.

'I'm sure her on the tenth floor is running a knocking shop. I mean, *I* don't mind what people get up to. I just wish her punters would wipe their bleeding feet on the doormat before they come into the building.'

She had the loudest voice I have ever heard in a woman; she spoke at a volume that one reserves to summon help in the event of being trapped at the bottom of a mineshaft.

My stint working in the film industry, this time behind the camera, came about when I was invited to help in the Wardrobe Department for a production company that specialised in television commercials.

Their star director, Brian Baderman, was a tall, thin, intense man who looked like a refugee from a European war film. His commercials had a very particular style that combined an off-kilter situationism with late 1960s modernist interiors. He never used professional actors but instead selected his cast from the Unemployment Office in Hackney, some of whom suffered with mental health problems.

He once cast the wife of Merthyr Tydfil's answer to Elvis, Shakin' Stevens. She was squat and wore her hair in a loose bun which bobbed about in perpetual motion on the crown of her head. Unexpectedly, she was a black belt Judo instructor who taught boys at a local youth centre.

'So,' she said, her feet firmly planted apart with a cigarette dangling from the corner of her mouth. 'I was in the *dojo* and I turned my back when one of them threw a flying kick at my head. But I've got a sixth sense, see? So, I did *this*.'

At which point, she flew into accelerated motor performance, simulating a complex manoeuvre of catching hold of someone's foot at the shoulder, jerking it up, kicking their other foot from beneath them and finally executing a *seoi otoshi*, a shoulder throw. This took only two seconds.

Brushing her hands together, she took the cigarette from her lips and blew a long plume into the air.

'*Don't* do that, Rudy.'

Well, I certainly wouldn't.

There followed three years in which I became a semi-respectable commuter, rising with everybody else and frequently being stranded on a Central Line train with revolting strangers due to signalling problems. It was difficult because doing anything *en masse* just goes against my nature, but it was necessary because there was no living to be earned in making music or in freelance writing. I felt that I was too mature to reinvent myself in the apprenticeship of a new role.

Possibly it's never too late to reinvent oneself, but I had no enthusiasm for it; my motivation was lacking. It seemed—and one had only to look at the circumstantial evidence—that any useful life in London was drawing to a close. My era was reaching its conclusion and the time had arrived for a new adventure, and a different view from a different armchair. In fact, it was imperative for my emotional and mental health because I was clinically depressed.

When one casually jokes about suicide it's a sign that something is fundamentally wrong. I am not sure when it began exactly, but it was gradual and strengthened by increments. Also, I began to drink heavily, which could not have helped. I felt impotent, powerless. I stopped working because I was unable to organise myself, especially first thing in the morning, and began to think of ways in which to end my life in as pain free a manner as possible.

It is difficult for people who have never experienced depression to understand this, but when one feels engulfed by the notion of utter pointlessness, human life quite literally goes down the plughole. One sees no point in *anything*. Depression is a merciless thief.

I considered the river. But drowning is an unpleasant death. An overdose or hanging was out, because I didn't want Paul to come home and find me dead in our home. One evening, which was almost Floridian—the air temperature was balmy and high winds arrived as if to herald a storm—I watched *Sombre* by Philippe Grandrieux, which no doubt urged me on, opened the living room window and climbed onto the window sill. I stood there, looking down at the car park, seventeen floors below.

I remembered that someone had tried to commit suicide many years before in Peckham. They threw themselves over a communal landing and ended up, very much alive, on the bonnet of car, but with their legs and arms dislocated. My neighbour, who saw it, told me that the survivor looked like 'an oven ready chicken'.

There is no way that anyone could survive the fall that I was contemplating, but then I thought, 'Someone is going to have to clear up the mess. And Paul, you can't do this to him. Imagine how he will feel. You *must* sort yourself out.'

There are many reasons why some of us become depressed, and each case is of course unique. For me, I think the root cause was that I felt that my life as a creative artist was over. I had not produced anything in quite a long time. It's a vicious circle, because depression robs you of motivation, which then leads to further despair at not having accomplished anything, and so on. Also, it is a tyranny that rules your life and, importantly, that of the partner who is doing his or her best to support you through it.

I rejected antidepressants after taking them for a month because they subtly shift you into a numb and detached dimension; wandering through the mechanics of daily life in a pharmaceutical fog; expressing neither opinions nor preferences; concentrating on spreading a pat of processed cheese towards all corners of a slice of toast. An automaton padding about in an unwashed dressing gown. You don't feel depressed, because you don't feel anything. I respect that antidepressants can help other people, but it wasn't for me. Perhaps I had been prescribed the wrong antidepressant, or too high a dosage. But, essentially, what I needed was change.

I decided to record again and collaborated with Peter Kinski in writing and recording the songs that came to be titled

The Milwaukee Sessions. Some of those songs, I feel, are quite beautiful, although they come from a very dark place; the voice is controlled, passionate and grave.

A little later I also collaborated with Noko of Apollo 440 and released *Born That Way* on the Sanctuary label. I felt that 'Born That Way' was the most perfect pop record I was ever likely to record, and together with the performance swansong at Earl's Court in London, it seemed a fitting epitaph to my life as a singer. Certainly, for the time being. It was a tremendous boost to my self-confidence and, slowly, the depression lifted.

Paul, also, wanted a change of scene and a change of pace, having grown weary of waking at four o'clock in the morning to drive to a film location, often in freezing conditions.

We put the flat on the market and it was sold within a week. Presentation must work, because as soon as the agent called to notify us that we had a viewing, I ran around kindling twenty-five tea lights and putting on Brian Eno's *The Plateaux of Mirror* before descending into Mr Sharma's Costcutter, thus 'keeping out of the way'.

We had two short, hectic months in which to make all the necessary arrangements and airlift ourselves out of this life and into the next. I boxed and sellotaped everything into storage, marking the chests with a series of numbers rather than clearly identifying their contents, as a precaution against theft. Later, I came to regret this, because I managed to lose the master list and was obliged to open everything to locate a complimentary travel sewing kit.

I was given an electric shredder with which to dispatch the paperwork of a former life. As children should not run whilst holding scissors, I should not be left alone with an electric shredder. I was so diligent with this machine—the GDR *Stasi* would have adored me—that, without realising, I destroyed both my birth certificate and Paul's driving licence. That's probably also where the master list disappeared to.

When the appointed morning arrived, the removal team came to take all our belongings to a storage facility until we were ready to send for them. That evening we held a farewell dinner with a few close friends in Shepherd's Bush. I invited my lawyer, whom I hardly knew, because I had some notion that, as a Holland Park boy, he would somehow have a social connection to my friends.

He did, they had mutual friends. But what I didn't know was that he was a chronic drinker turned Alcoholics Anonymous zealot who attended meetings nightly. He told us his story, and his struggle, to a table of eyes meditating on a repast of pork medallions before accidentally lodging a leg of his chair through a hole in the wooden flooring, collapsing backwards and sprawling on the floor. Fully sober, of course, to experience the humiliation. Poor man.

The following morning, we returned to the flat to collect our suitcases. Paul made himself scarce and attended to practical matters. Is the water and electricity properly disconnected? Are all the cupboards free of any incriminating evidence?

I stood at the window of the empty living room, in a sort of reverie, having a private moment. I, it should be said, used to suffer with nostalgia in both legs. Looking out at the view and the horizon of a West London I had adopted as my home for the past seven years, and which I had come to know so well, the memories flooded back.

The time that Paul, with umpteen yards of copper organza and a staple gun, enthusiastically dressed the long hallway. Our neighbours came for dinner and thought they had walked into a twenty-foot-long coffin.

The leafy streets of Chiswick, where I once met the British actress Fenella Fielding coming out of Tesco Metro. She was wearing a tartan suit and pushing a shopping trolley customised in the same material. She was erect and unapproachable, the hair an impregnable helmet. I went to speak to her but she froze me with a look that said, 'Do not touch. One small nudge and my pelvic girdle will come crashing down to the pavement.'

The Uxbridge Road, the venue of so many dinners, parties and celebrations, especially at the long, century-old wooden table of our friend Judy. The same table at which I auditioned for *Middleton's Changeling*.

Goodbye to Richmond and its Thames River Path, along which I would sometimes walk all the way from Hammersmith to Hampton Court. Twelve miles, I imagine. Walking is good, because it is a natural pace by which to travel, and gives one time to think, to ponder, to contemplate.

Goodbye to Kew and its botanical gardens. And, finally, goodbye to Holland Park.

NUEVA VIDA,
NUEVA AVENTURA

ON A CLEAR MAY MORNING. I stood on the bow of the car ferry *Berlioz* watching the white cliffs of Dover recede into the distance and, with it, the past and quite a sizeable carbon footprint. Since the *Berlioz* was, alas, a car ferry and not a motor yacht, we drove south towards the sun. Through France, over the Pyrenees, which is both a mountain range and a giant draught excluder, and into Spain.

I am a Hispanophile since my earliest memories. As a child, when occasionally we used to go on holiday to Fleetwood in Lancashire, to stay with my mother's family, all conversation would have to cease for five minutes while I mounted the table, wearing a sombrero, and danced to *Granada*. I would then descend to silence and befuddlement. Where this passion for Spain originates, I do not truthfully know.

Many people who have been to Spain do not know it at all. Once you leave the big cities or the urbanised nightmare of its coastal holding pens, you enter a continent. Rugged sierras, Celtic landscapes in the North West, a vast ironing board plain at its centre and, in Andalusia, a desert.

The Spanish who live on the eastern coast, the Levante, are a Mediterranean people whose history and culture are shaped by French and Italian influences. They are, generally, a relaxed people. They are very open, given to acts of kindness, courteous, helpful with strangers, patient, pragmatic and they love their fiestas. Occasionally, you might see windmilling of the arms and shouting, which passes for normal speech, but they're not quite as excitable as their brothers across the sea, the Neapolitans.

They value their traditions and customs, which have prevailed for centuries, because it is the adhesive of identity and it binds both a people, and families together. The Valencians and the Catalans, as in other parts of Spain, see their regional culture, their regional identity—and, sometimes, language— as predominant over nationality. Or, rather, over Madrid. When speaking of Spain, one is speaking of seventeen autonomous communities unified by the nation state. Galicia and Andalucía, Catalonia and Extremadura are very distinct; a distinction which is not defined by geography alone.

On driving into Spain, one sees the difference immediately. France is green; Spain is red. From the air, the patchwork quilt is quite different. France is somehow more ordered, manicured, reined in; its fields are perfect little green stamps. The other side of the Pyrenees, it is wilder, drier, more expansive, and the agriculture is different.

On the ground and travelling by car, another distinction can be seen on a human scale: motorway service cafes and bars. French ones hum with silence; travellers consult their Michelin or inspect the *petits cadeaux regionaux* gift stand with mild curiosity. In Spain, you must shout your order above the din of a turbine air fan cranked up to full throttle, and two televisions tuned into different stations at maximum volume.

There is a little generalisation here, but I feel not much.

We bought a townhouse in need of complete renovation close to the Valencian town of Xàtiva, which nestles at the foot of the Monte Bernisa. Outside of the Córdoba-Seville triangle known as the *sartén* (the frying pan), it is one of the hottest parts of Spain. It might have been nice had someone told us this when we first embarked on a renovation in August: four floors with a roof terrace and sixty-eight steps.

We engaged a small, diligent team of Transylvanian builders to demolish unwanted walls and put new beams into place. There was a dilapidated roof to the rear of the house which we converted into a secondary terrace. The paperwork involved in such a venture is a bureaucrat's multiple orgasm. For months, we lived in comparative yet picturesque squalor.

The downstairs bathroom—a dank, dark and forbidding place which did not encourage one to linger—was without the vital furniture of a door. So, I was obliged to recirculate a limited repertoire of music hall favourites, including Alfred Tennyson's 'Come into The Garden, Maude' and Marie Lloyd's relentless 'A Little of What You Fancy', until privacy was reinstalled.

I mention this to illustrate that, in the beginnings of renovation, even the most private of moments are not guaranteed without a builder barging in.

It was a courageous undertaking because neither of us had any previous experience of renovating a house, and our ignorance of that undertaking was bliss. I could barely hang wallpaper.

A full electrical rewiring was essential because the previous owners were using exposed bell wire that was decades old. Within the first few weeks of moving in, we had visitors who came to stay for their annual holiday. The gravity of the electrical arrangement was highlighted when I blithely flicked on a kettle in the kitchen at the precise moment that a guest plugged in some curling tongs, and short-circuited dinner.

All the walls had to be laboriously scraped before we began to plaster. As layer upon layer were chiselled away, the house told its story and, with it, the revelation that at some point during the 1960s, a family member had taken a night school paint effects class. The burden of stripping the walls back to their original surface mainly fell to me, because I exhibited no talent for plastering. Plastering is not unlike cake decoration, it really is all in the wrist action.

The large attic space at the top of the house, which would adjoin the new terrace, was home to a wasps' nest and a small colony of bats which had to be professionally removed before making it into a habitable space. I booked an appointment to have my teeth scraped that day.

The floors were all re-laid with plain, sand-coloured tiling which took months to complete because there is not a proper right angle in the whole of the province. The electric cutting of tiles and the fine ceramic dust that it produces, which stays airborne for months and creeps into every conceivable corner of one's life, was a battle of nerves that almost did me in.

Finally arriving at the painting stage was a breakthrough and the thought of painting a four-storey house felt not like a chore, but a relief. But, amid the toil and the sweat there were moments of accomplishment and satisfaction.

We learnt, too late, that one should never live amid the early stages of a renovation because the debris alone will conspire to systematically shred you to the last fibre of human tolerance. It is impossible to wear contact lenses or to accept any invitations that require clean clothes. Everywhere we went, we left a deposit of dust in our wake.

To further illustrate this, one evening, in the kitchen, Paul and I had an actual, physical confrontation. He lunged at me, his hands around my throat—which I daresay a few people might have enjoyed—and I swiped his glasses off his face. I broke free. There was an interlude where I refused to come out of the bathroom. And then we sat down on bags of *yeso*, Spanish plaster, and got very drunk.

Old houses require continual upkeep because there are nearly always recurring problems like damp, and they can become your mistress. Having left the confines of a one-bedroomed flat in London to live in a space of 200 square metres, a prospect at which one might almost *pirouette* with joy, there are considerations. Spain is a very dusty country: when the wind comes from the south it imports Saharan sand and deposits everything with a fine film of Algerian ferrous red.

All those ceramic floors must be mopped at the very least once a week and, although I don't wish to carp, I was up and down the stairs with a fresh bucket like a Victorian scullery maid. It did wonders for my waistline and buttocks, but I feared that much more wear and tear on the knees and I'd be paying my rates bill from a motorised wheelchair.

One saw them quite often, whizzing around town, and at first I had assumed that they were the common result of hiking accidents in the nearby sierra. But now I know that it's the stairs. Therefore, with advancing years, the Spanish abandon the upper floors of their homes and live solely on the ground floor.

The neighbours were very welcoming. On the summer evening that we first took possession, they were sitting out in the street to take the air and exchange rumours, when we marched past them lugging a king-size mattress. They were the mafiosa of our street, presided over by The Big Broom. The Big Broom had sired eleven children and her eldest, the Deputy Big Broom was being groomed to eventually occupy The Big Wickerwork Chair. There was Carmen, whose son was a tidal wave of camp that engulfed anything in its path, yet whom everybody fully expected to marry. And there was Mendieta.

Mendieta's forty-something son still lived with her. Acting on a city ordinance that electricity meters must be installed into the façade of the house, he borrowed a masonry drill—which was the size of a harpoon—from some itinerant Romanians. Through the course of an hour he excavated a hole that would have accommodated a new bay window. We all stood on our balconies impassively watching his progress, and waiting for the finale when his mother awoke from her siesta.

It never occurred to anyone to wrest this instrument of destruction from his hands; in Spain, death and disaster are spectator sports. Live action is far better than a telenovela.

On the evening of our first arrival, deciding to quash any debate and meet them head-on, we introduced ourselves bearing a tray of amontillado. The Spanish are not particularly prejudiced against males who cohabit if they can identify who takes the "male" and who takes the "female" roles.

Lesbian couples fare somewhat differently. To be in possession of a fully functioning pair of ovaries, yet to remain obstinately childless, is construed as an outright rejection of the Virgin Mary.

I was assigned the female role because it was I who swept the front step and pavement. The fast track to integration here is not necessarily in developing your language skills but, rather, to stand outside your house with a broom and look busy for ten minutes on a twice-weekly basis.

'El inglés is sweeping the pavement again.'

'Sí.'

'He is a clean person.'

'Sí.'

'Clean boy.'

'Not dirty like her at number 7.'

'No. She is a dirty, *dirty* bitch.'

'But he is clean.'

'Sí.'

'Look, he's mopping the front step.'

'Sí.'

The street bleaching business can be highly competitive and, once entered into, you lapse at your peril.

Integrating oneself into Spanish society can be difficult. As I have said, it is not simply a question of learning the language, where having mastered it to a sufficient level one may expect immediately to be surrounded by new friends. It is more rooted, as in any relationship, on having things in common.

In Madrid or Barcelona, there exists a certain accessibility because you're in the bustle of a cosmopolitan city where foreigners are a significant minority, and part of the fabric of everyday life. On the coasts, where there are high concentrations of Northern Europeans, attachments are generally formed between fellow countrymen and women. It's easier, not only because of the language but, importantly, because one has a shared experience. And that is the nub.

If you live neither in a principal city nor on the coast, it can be more difficult. Overall, the Spanish are easy-going and friendly, but acquaintances cannot become friends unless you can move beyond a superficial level of mutuality. In essence, if you were born and raised in London, what do you have in common with someone whose prime concern is olives and oranges?

However, we chose to live in the "real Spain", and away from the Costas.

I harboured no wish to join a community of expats, or the clubs and groups which they form. Many, with hours and hours of leisure time stretching before them, invariably turn to all day tippling and gossip-mongering. About *you*.

The small expat community was alerted that a celebrity had moved into the area. Anyone that has glanced through my royalty statements knows that I could never be described as a celebrity. Dinner invitations followed, as did a volley of personal and financial questions. The answers were then telegraphed.

I was sidled up to at the fish counter of a local supermarket by a stranger, who asked, 'So what is Morrissey *really* like?' The drawbridge went up.

There was a very brief acquaintanceship with a gay male couple who had moved from London into a villa outside town. Their neighbours, who were English and Christian, had a clear view of them frolicking in their swimming pool and were trying to denounce them at the town hall. Eventually, it proved to no avail; there is no specific law against having sex on one's own property and grounds.

Their cavorting was popular knowledge, and I thought that someone should inform them, so that they could meet with their neighbours and resolve any dispute. So, I told them, on Christmas Eve, as they were dressing their tree. The following morning, they went to speak with their neighbours, who vehemently denied everything.

That evening, I received a telephone call from the taller partner, who I will call "The Taller One Who Seems Placid But Is In Fact Quite Volatile", while the shorter partner, "The Theatrical One Who Overdoes It At Christmas" was weeping in the background.

'You're trying to ruin our new life! You're trying to destroy our New Dawn!'

Destroyer of New Dawns. I was too flattered to argue with him.

The Spanish do not really believe in the idea of having best friends. It's an Anglo-Saxon or Teutonic concept. Here, everything is done in groups. You do not meet *a* friend to go to the cinema, you meet *several* friends. Southern Europeans are more group-oriented and I think this is a legacy of the Roman Catholic Church. Group activity is safe, provided you're not planning a *coup*. But people who pair off in duos, and whom are not engaged to be married, are subject to a degree of suspicion. It goes against the Mediterranean tradition for two people of the same sex to spend too much time together, regardless of their sexuality.

'Alberto and Oscar were seen in the square again last night.'

'What were they doing?'

'There were no girls at the table, yet they were *enjoying* themselves.'

Spaniards can be part of the same group of friends all their lives: from the infant's school playground, all the way to the melamine counter where one draws one's pension. So, forming a friendship with a Spaniard—the question of mutuality apart—can be complicated by the simple fact that they probably have no need of you. It's not a manifestation of arrogance or rejection.

When some do encounter the effusive and profoundly loyal notion of a northern European style "best friendship", they are delighted if not a little disoriented by it. To have attention heaped on you by someone who is neither your wife, husband nor child is an alien experience. Close bonding is generally limited to family.

Spontaneity is thin on the ground. It is, in the main, reserved for party-throwing gypsies. Life is an inflexible timetable structured around meal times, of which there are five: el desayuno (breakfast), tapas (elevenses), la comida (lunch), la merienda (snack) and la cena (dinner). In summer, when the mercury rises, it is not unusual to see people out and about at two o'clock in the morning, looking for a *churrería* (hot chocolate and doughnut stand) before finally submitting to the bolster. Spanish towns are full of pale-faced children running around, trying to lose energy, so that they may sleep.

The Spanish are so consistent in their daily movements that the country is a contract killer's bonanza in terms of ease of elimination. Even I had become predictable: I went to the supermarket at 3PM sharp during the siesta period because to do otherwise is to participate in the panic outbreak of a Balkan war.

Returning to spontaneity, or the lack of it: seemingly everything must be arranged in advance. Yet, ironically, if you want to get a Spaniard to agree to a fixed time you may, depending on whom you're dealing with, enter into an absurd pantomime. They will often defer confirmation until the last possible minute. It's quite perplexing. My own thought is that readily agreeing to an appointment at an advanced date interferes with a certain, characteristic *inertia*.

Inertia is the only way I can describe it. I don't mean laziness, but rather a disinclination to make a commitment. If you're someone who likes to organise everything on a wall chart, you have two choices: either yield to life, or become mute with frustration.

I was quite surprised to find that many Spanish no longer smoke. Moreover, many do not drink either, beyond perhaps a cocktail taken in a bar at the weekend, which is sipped in a sort of mime of actual drinking.

'I am in a cocktail bar therefore I should have *a* cocktail, with *several* friends.'

This is a variation on another Spanish custom: 'The calendar says we are not quite in May, so even though it is 25 degrees outside, I must still wear a scarf.' Tradition can sometimes be bound up with a certain rigidness, which is how it remains "tradition".

One must wonder how there are so many bars in a country of modest imbibers. Coffee. They drink coffee, right up to bedtime. Of course, there are exceptions. If you visit a truck stop at six in the morning, you'll see lorry drivers knee-deep in cigarette butts and discarded anchovy wrappers knocking back cognacs before taking to the nation's highways. These to me are the real Spanish: untouched by The Hague and EU legislation.

Cocaine usage is widespread, yet to amble the streets while intoxicated is a social taboo; a stranger is likely to tell you to pull yourself together.

My next-door neighbours invited me to an alfresco family dinner at their *casita* outside town. They were extremely hospitable and kind, but we all sat around a long table for three hours with a large bottle of Coca Cola in the middle of it. We chatted about many things but all the while there was a cartoon bubble over my head with the question: 'When is someone going to crack open a bottle?'

Of course, once dinner was served there was wine, which hardly anybody touched and which I finished. I was then brought a decorative bottle of locally produced firewater and a shot glass. When I asked whether anyone was going to join me in a tasting, I received the reply, 'Oh no. It was more of an ornament, really.'

The Spanish are not solitary creatures and it is almost impossible to be left to one's own devices for long before being abducted and carried to a table of roast suckling pig. Vegetarianism is considered an affliction. Announcing one's vegetarianism translates as meaning that you can eat *wafer-thin* ham. Any country that has known starvation within living memory prizes flesh. In the street, one may see mothers forcing food into the upturned, unwilling mouths of weeping children who are simply unable to digest any more calories.

One year, I was asked to speak with a group of advanced English language students at a nearby adult education college. The premise was a topical discussion and an exchange of ideas. We spoke, in a very general way, about the transformation of Spain from a dictatorship to an emerging, modern democracy in the period following Franco's death in 1975. Spain, in the latter quarter of the 20th century, rapidly transformed itself at a level that is quite astonishing. And one of the sectors that would change Spain forever was tourism, with a consequent boom in the construction industry, and its reinvention as the California of Europe.

At the end of that discussion, what transpired was an agreement on a singular, collective image of modernisation: hard porn was prominently displayed next to children's comics in the street kiosks of the country's cities and towns (usually staffed by sexagenarian matrons).

As the British experienced the sea change of social and sexual liberation during the 1960s through to the 1980s, Spain's journey towards modernisation began almost twenty years later. As we had The Beatles, Twiggy, Mary Quant, David Bailey and Monty Python, Spain had *La Movida,* in the 1980s, a Madrid-based artistic movement which bore the country's most successful international film director, Pedro Almodóvar.

A friend of mine who studied Spanish at Valladolid while David Bowie's *Aladdin Sane* tore through the Hit Parade told me that he saw malnutrition: barefoot children, their clothes in rags, playing football, and a society policed by the feared *grises* (Franco's enforcers). Under Franco, wives were not permitted to travel across provincial borders without the written consent of their husbands. Then, the Maghreb began not at Tangier but south of the Pyrenees.

With the coming of emancipation through the legislature of human rights, Spain has one of the highest divorce rates in Europe. But, then, feminism has come late to this country. It was also one of the very first countries in the world that sanctioned gay marriage. Not civil unions, but marriage.

As most Spaniards are Roman Catholic this might be surprising, but after the sociopathic double act of Isabella and Ferdinand, the Inquisition and the dictatorship of *El Caudillo*, it has bred an attitude of anticlericalism, if not anti-authoritarianism. Spain is a country of Catholics, but it is not a Catholic country.

After an occupation that lasted 700 years, the Moors were finally expelled back to North Africa, together with Sephardic Jews, in a *reconquista* that fully Catholicised Spain. One of its legacies, apart from decorative ceramics, enticing patios and the gift of irrigation—without which Spain would now be a classifiable desert—is the absence of spices in the cuisine and the surprising fact that one must request a pepper cellar in a restaurant.

Historically, to season one's dishes with spices was discouraged; it was perceived as anti-Catholic, or pro-Islamic. Therefore, a spicy Sicilian repast with its robust, North African flavours would surprise a native of Segovia.

I think it could be said that in the Spanish psyche exists a preoccupation with death. Contrary to the northern European fear of eventual expiry, the Spanish attitude to death is almost Arabic in its passive fatalism. Death is not merely inseparable from life, it is vital to it. So much so that I maintain that the national sport here is neither football nor bullfighting, but overtaking other drivers whilst on the brow of a hill. The road accident rate is appalling, but when a Hispanic male straps himself into the cockpit of his Seat Córdoba, it is not motoring, it is a mission. Machismo.

This unconcealed attraction to death is not borne of a blood-thirstiness or barbarism but, rather, it is more of an enthralled curiosity. It is difficult to explain but, simplistically, I liken it to the experience of intently watching one's partner as they abandon volition during intense lovemaking, and reaching climax, surrender and *release*. That, in any case, is how I interpret it.

I have never attended a bullfight, which remains popular here, especially in the south, and have no desire to do so. Not least because the outcome is always certain, and the bull may never win. They are screened on national television on Sundays and one observes how, on occasions when the matador is out-manoeuvred and tossed into the air with a horn impaled in his coccyx, the cameras zoom in on the bloodshed, and his agony is detailed in slow motion playback.

I have been to a bull run, where the bulls are freed from the corral to thunder through the streets—young men running ahead of them—and once witnessed a goring. A rather over-weight man's buttocks were repeatedly charged at against the door of a pharmacy. Unfortunately, they were closed at the time (the pharmacy, not his buttocks). As he banged on the security grille, crying, 'Help me! *Help me* for God's sake!' everybody just stood and gawped.

And I, too, watched in frozen fascination, captivated by afternoon violence. So, perhaps, a part of me was becoming Spanish.

The idea that Spain is one long, continual *paseo* of tapas bars, sauntering along a promenade, wearing a vermilion impulse purchase, as if one were living in a perpetual Indian summer, is untrue. Outside of the major cities, Spain, literally, closes. It doesn't close as much as France, whose towns and villages during the off-peak months give the impression of the outcome of a nuclear winter.

But, in the winter months, it feels at times as if one might as well be living in Bolton, in 1971, except without the highlight of Diana Coupland in *Spring and Port Wine*. The bars and the streets are empty, save for leaves rustling and gathering in large clumps by the gutters, driven by a stealthy wind from La Mancha.

Spring and summer, which is a long season, is different. Everything comes alive. Colour re-enters the calendar. I have a theory that all Spanish men must own the same shirt because, one summer, there was a mass break out of fuchsia. *Everybody* bought a fuchsia shirt.

The skies blaze, with almost uninterrupted certainty, day after day. The sun is so intense that it is impossible to leave the house without sunglasses, especially given whitewashed surroundings. One moves with the rhythm of the sun: rising early to escape the late morning heat, to do one's chores or business, sleeping in the afternoon and dining late, sometimes at midnight, when the temperatures are more comfortable.

August means *fiesta*, or more accurately the week-long celebration of the *Moros y Cristianos*, the Moors and Christians. Months beforehand, everybody practises their musical instruments, designs their costumes and plans their makeup to take their part in the processions.

The first time I saw this spectacle, the band began their march down the main avenue when the heavens opened and there was a sudden deluge. Violently rained on by hailstones, drenched and with running eye makeup, the parade disintegrated and the liberating 'Christian army' rapidly took on the appearance of an Alice Cooper fans' convention.

That is the one time of year that you may get drunk in public, fire weapons into the sky, and set a match to anything incendiary. It is not surprising to see one's own bank manager staggering around a corner, looking lost in little but a pair of tights and a boob tube.

When people ask you how life is they might say, 'How is it progressing?' Progress is the assumption that life moves ineluctably forward. Time moves forward, but life doesn't always necessarily follow. Sometimes, it can spin into reverse.

It strikes me that, in a sense, I had returned to a "Bermondsey" of my youth. But a Bermondsey with mantillas. Living in a street where neighbours greet each other and sit outside to take the air on warm summer evenings; where a child who discovers the unique annoyance of pressing a doorbell before running away is likely to end up with comprehensively slapped legs; and where I could be found alone in my room, tapping out words to the opening chapter of this memoir on the modern equivalent of a Smith Corona typewriter.

SOIRÉES OF TERPSICHORE

THE TWO FRIENDSHIPS I HAD in Xàtiva, in the *comarca*, ended. One of them terminated very abruptly, and the other I discontinued for my own sanity.

G. was single, in his early forties and originally from Cornwall. We didn't have an awful lot in common, but certainly enough for me to "swing round" in the early evening for a chat and a few glasses of wine before returning home for dinner. Occasionally, we made an excursion to the coast: I was the owner of a car, but without a driver's licence, and he was a motorist without a vehicle.

G. was formerly a website designer and, from time to time, he repaired computers for the British expat community who lived in what was called the *extrarradio*: the outlying districts. Quite a grand term for a town of fifty thousand people, one normally associates it with Madrid or Mexico City. At the time of knowing him, I was so absorbed in the writing of this book that, one day, I didn't notice that the town was almost encircled by raging forest fires. I was experimenting with a new font when a friend in Albacete telephoned me, after seeing the early evening news. I suppose the townspeople didn't notify me because, quite logically, they thought that a cineaste would be of no use in a municipal emergency.

For quite some time I laboured under the illusion that all Spaniards adore the films of Pedro Almodóvar and, further, harbour an unquenchable desire to discuss them. At a dinner, I once met a Spaniard who did not like his films. Naturally, on learning this, our conversation was swiftly concluded.

G. had a lot of time on his hands. He spent most days logged on to various internet dating sites in the hope that someone would travel to see him. Many did, although I believe few returned. There's nothing wrong with living life as a sexual safari; but I think it's only good manners to offer one's visitor a beer and a tapa, especially if they've driven fifty miles. A bit of a scoot around with a mop and some fresh sheets doesn't go amiss either, particularly in a hot and dusty climate.

One morning, G. appeared at my door looking extremely agitated. On waking and taking his small dog out for a walk, he discovered that the local town hall had installed a chrome bin directly onto the façade of his house. As he quite rightly complained, they had done this without his prior permission. He asked me if I would accompany him to the town hall as a translator. By then, I was virtually fluent in Spanish and without attending a single language lesson. I had simply thrown myself into the process of integration with the alacrity of an Olympic runner. However, visiting the town hall was not something to be relished, let alone on someone else's behalf, because dealing with Spanish officialdom often results in skin conditions that require a topical ointment to clear up. Nonetheless, I agreed and accompanied him to his house.

It *was* scandalous. They had installed a piece of municipal furniture no more than a metre from his door. Moreover, as his house was situated on a corner, they could have easily and less offensively placed it on the blank, side façade of his house. I decided to be both pragmatic and to introduce a little humour into the situation. Mindful of the fact that he regularly received visitors, I said to him:

'Let's not be in a mad dash to go to the town hall. If you think about it, they have done you a favour. When your guests leave, they can simply deposit the used condom in the bin provided, before returning to wherever they came from. It's actually convenient.'

We never spoke again. I returned home, disconnected the phone and poached myself an egg. While it was true that I had seemingly lost a friend, I had also spared myself an eczema outbreak on the ankles just as the shorts season was approaching.

The other friend in question was a retired colonel and *padre* in the British army. He had seen active service in Bosnia where, accidentally, or so he claimed, he was shot at by his own side. He was a good man, although he harboured a number of peculiarities, some of which were more endearing than others.

In social situations, he was possessed of a pathological drive to be the centre of attention—and to remain there—at any cost. In order to maintain this position, his behaviour would gradually pass from mild eccentricity to aggressive pedestrianism. This is the mark of those who have come to the end of their repertoire, yet who refuse to pass the baton. Thus, at a certain point in the evening, he would often metamorphose into the persona of a Jamaican dancehall queen from North Peckham who enjoys sticking her bum out to Aretha Franklin. His bum—which I certainly held no interest in—was both ubiquitous and, at times, undesirably close.

I did wonder whether it was a form of sexual assault through a forced voyeurism on the part of dinner guests. In any case, I simply put it down to the *after-effects of warfare*. However, in fairness, I must admit that I have been guilty of attempting Flamenco dance at the fag-end of a party, skidding off-course, disappearing behind a room divider and emerging, disoriented, on a Juliet balcony. Knowing him occasionally brought me into contact with the expat community, which I generally avoided.

One of the colonel's friends was Iris Elliott. Iris was a retired BBC wardrobe manager who threw *Soirées of Terpsichore* in the garden of her villa. She was an unpublished novelist and an unstaged dancer. Her husband, Raymond, wore his coloured hair with an exaggerated wave at the front and favoured the polka-dot neck scarf. He was always stationed at her elbow, her comfort and requirement his utmost concern, perpetually engaged in the pantomime of illogical fuss.

'A cushion?'

'A cushion.'

Until they were properly introduced as husband and wife, one surmised that he was a homosexual companion of many years standing. I wasn't alone in this assumption: seeing the wedding ring on her finger, and taking the man stood next to her to be an effete amanuensis, a well-meaning soul had asked her, 'When did your husband pass away?'

These soirées were often themed in the sense that guests were encouraged to adopt fancy dress. This bore little relation to the evening's programme, but rather was an ex-wardrobe manager's way of having people make an effort. At the evening I attended the theme was "oriental" and, on arriving, it looked like a fez wearers' convention. The male guests were grouped together and drifting about the garden, like disoriented Ottomans in search of a mothership. The women were more flamboyantly attired as belly-dancers and courtesans, although one guest arrived in a length of hessian sacking. It was difficult to tell whether she had come as a Parthian prostitute, or a vintage bottle of Port.

If you have ever witnessed that peculiarly British natural disaster known as "Am-Dram", then you will know that its success depends entirely upon a common access of good will, not good acting. An oleander tree was studded with a great many twinkling lights and a soft, warm breeze enveloped us. Raymond, coiffed and draped in an embroidered kaftan of midnight blue, circulated bearing a tray of amontillado before we settled down on rugs laid across the lawn.

A person of very short stature recited a very long piece of poetry which comprised an endless serving of inspirational quotes: 'A dark cloud is just a silver cloud turned inside out!' Well that's nice to know. 'Death is merely the departure hall to a celestial arrivals lounge!' Clearly, she had never travelled with a budget airline.

Next, we had a tenor who performed an aria. He did not sing it, but gamely set about it like an avuncular family butcher, dispatching each stanza as if it were a cut from a whole side of pork. The aria was not known to me; or, I might well have known it but his rendition obfuscated any recognition.

Far more recognisable was the dramatic and foreboding

overture of Prokofiev's 'Montagues and Capulets' that presaged the appearance of our host, Iris. In a lavish, brightly coloured silk robe and a headdress decorated with peacock plumes, our Scheherazade emerged from the darkness of a small olive grove to our left. Swaying to the motoric rhythm, she drew ever closer before planting herself before us. From the confines of her long black wig, which hung either side of her face like Swish curtains, her eyes were fixed on the distant Moon above us. My neighbour, a Scottish woman called June, nudged me and unnecessarily clarified, 'Moon.' I looked over to the colonel, who seemed to be enjoying it immensely. Then the dance began.

Interpretative dance is a mystery to me, but it's my impression that she was conveying the ascent of Ancient Egypt—the fingertips pressed together with the palms separated symbolising the erection of pyramids—followed by its demise (she nimbly ran a circuit around us as if in a flight of terror). Abruptly, she threw herself to the ground where she thrashed about, moaning. We watched impassively, sipping amontillado, as the moaning then gave way to howling and petitions. I assumed that it was part of the story and that perhaps we had moved on to the First Punic War. In fact, she was in the grip of a sudden and very severe cramp.

Raymond was in the kitchen preparing canapés when he heard her. Rushing out from the house, he seized hold of her left foot and raised her leg vertically.

'Cushion!' he demanded.

'Montagues and Capulets', on repeat play, was still blaring out in fortissimo as a spectator's circle of fez wearers surrounded them. I thought it only polite to ask if I could do anything, which went unheard. He'd obviously done this before because, in releasing Iris from her muscle spasm, Raymond, workmanlike, manipulated the heel of her foot back and forth in the mechanical movement of an oil derrick in full production.

'Iris! Iris! Iris!'

'It's the *other* fucking leg!' she cried.

A few weeks afterwards, I was dining with the colonel. There had been a medical emergency, followed by consultations at which he acted as translator. It transpired that Iris had been drinking upwards of a bottle of brandy a day for thirty years, hence the violent cramps. She had died four days previously.

'She hadn't been sober since 1986. Nobody knew. She was a functioning alcoholic. I had to tell them that her organs were liquefying. *Licuándose.*'

'How awful. But what happened in 1986?', I asked.

'She'd written a novel. Raymond said it was marvellous, but then he adored her. Anyway, it was rejected. So, she burnt it in the garden.'

'In the Garden of Terpsichore.'

'Yes, you could say that. I suppose there are some things that you never get over. Very sad. More hotpot?'

LAST EXIT TO VALENCIA

TWO YEARS AFTER OUR COSTLY RENOVATION of the house, which, by then, we knew we had bought at an inflated price, the money began to run out. Eventually, it does. However, I am virtually unemployable: publishing is not an industry that one enters if one wishes to make money, especially nowadays. As a recording artist I belong, apparently, to a niche market. In retrospect, it was unreasonable to expect that we would never have to work again. Our plan, like others before us, was to renovate houses, sell them on, and live modestly off the profits. But, in 2008, came the economic crash.

Paul returned to England, to work in the film industry, living in shared quarters, while I maintained the house in Spain, doing everything I could to promote and sell it.

So began long periods of separation, often for months. To be separated from one's partner for such periods can be difficult, but it was he who had made the necessary sacrifice, not I, and so one's attitude was pragmatic, and one simply gets on with it in a spirit of faith. However, the dynamic changes. One is not sharing a home anymore; one is not living the envisaged dream. Rather, one is caretaking a shared memory. Without being mawkish about it, the experience of sitting on a terrace of plants you have lovingly tended is somewhat diminished by the fact that one is infrequently able to share it.

Worthy of recount is an incident that happened to Paul on one of his journeys home. He boarded the Stansted Express early in the morning to catch a flight out. As they were hurtling at great speed through Hertfordshire, someone threw themselves from the top of an embankment into the path of the oncoming train. A few seats away from Paul, a woman in a pink jumpsuit and pink, tasselled ankle boots—with matching overhead luggage—was sat, slack-jawed, staring out of the window. Previously, she had been speaking volubly on her iPhone about her impending holiday.

Suddenly, the driver of the train hit the brakes and it came to a grinding, coffee-splashing halt. As this happened, part of a man's face containing the eye splattered onto the window directly in front of her and, kept there by suction, slowly inched across it. The man who jumped. At this horrific interruption of her daydream, she became hysterical and ran down the carriage, screaming. Paul said it was like being in a Hammer film, *Horror Train*.

At the other end of the carriage, a female passenger who bore a resemblance to Hattie Jaques grabbed the screaming woman and mercilessly slapped her about the face, presumably to bring her out of shock. There is, of course, quite a difference between one firm slap and a sustained violent assault.

When the police and emergency services arrived, everybody had to exit the train. "Pink jumpsuit" was sedated and taken away on a stretcher. We don't know what happened to her matching luggage. Luckily, at that time, there were two daily flights to Valencia, so Paul could continue his journey. He polished off the better part of a bottle of whiskey that evening.

When Paul left, in the winter, it felt odd to be alone. I'm no stranger to being alone, but this was a solitariness in new circumstances. Solitariness can be contained if you live in a flat, or apartment, but a large house can yawn with emptiness if you're not careful. I did not live in a bustling city such as Valencia—90 kilometres distant—so I had to find my own distractions.

I made a new friend through social media. José-María. José-María lived in Valencia, with his partner. His family lived in a small town approximate to mine. As with many Spanish, he carried out his familial obligations assiduously, visiting his elderly parents to do chores and, sometimes, to harvest the crop on the land that they owned. He would make the one-hour journey south every two weeks to spend the weekend with them, and would pass the Friday afternoon or evening with me. I began to learn Valenciano, which is a dialect of Catalan and native to the *Comunidad Valenciana*, although some Valencianos argue that it is a distinct language.

Sometimes we would sit on the roof terrace at dusk, watching the frenzied aerial ballet of swallows swooping above our heads, feeding on the wing. When I lived in London, I had only a window box, so the prospect of suddenly having outside space transformed me into a zealous container gardener. I didn't stop at pots of flowers or small shrubs: I remember Paul heaving a nine-foot Yucca tree and bags of earth up to the top of the house, panting like an overheated Polar bear. I did help — I didn't just stand there directing, with a Fortuna cigarette between my fingers. I became thoroughly used to insects, allowing wasps to crawl over my fingers, and Carpenter bees to buzz around me, without running into the house with all the grace of a twelve year-old girl with unresolved orthodontic problems.

The terrace required twice-daily watering during the summer months, when the temperature was a meringue oven setting. I was the irrigation system. Effectively, it meant that I could not leave from May until October. I was trapped in an abusive relationship with a *Photinia Japonica* that sulked every time I left the house. If this were going to happen to me, I would much rather it be with Robert Mitchum in *Cape Fear*.

Although now a city-dweller, José-María was raised in the countryside and advised me on planting, or more specifically, what not to plant if one were to avoid expense and tears. Unfortunately, his arrival into my life was a little too late.

'It can plunge to minus 3 degrees in winter and rise to 40 degrees in summer. There's no shade here. Yucca, cactus and succulents.'

'But I have vine and jasmine. And if I want to go to London?'

'Then go to London, but when you return only the yucca will have survived. Everything else will die.'

'That's very stark.'

'But then you *did* fall out with the only friend who was willing to come up here and water them.' He was referring to G. around the corner, he of the municipal condom disposal unit.

During one of his visits, we decided to dine at a local Italian restaurant. On entering, we were shown to a table placed in clear view of a British couple from the Midlands. I had met them briefly before. The husband was an electrician who proudly boasted of having fitted their villa with British three-pin sockets—which is akin to erecting a *Gone with the Wind* staircase in a Sidcup bungalow—and his wife was a martyr to menopausal hot flushes who complained at the lack of an independent income. It was humourously suggested to her that, as we lived in a climate where alfresco dining was possible well into December, she rent herself out as a space heater on the terraces of restaurants.

Baldly, they stared at me while I refused to acknowledge them. After fifteen minutes, I decided to show them what I do with my bread while waiting for the starter to arrive. I pour equal amounts of olive oil and vinegar on a side plate, season it with pepper and use it as a dip for the bread. I believe it is an Andalusian habit which I probably picked up in the late 1980s, along with the prodigious use of Elnett and making large statements.

As I dunked the bread, I looked over at them and winked, inviting them to share in this custom of mine. However, my wink must have derailed from the culinary conspiratorial to the brazenly solicitous, because her eyebrows shot up towards the fresco-by-numbers ceiling and she turned to her husband, pelting him with whispers. José-María, meanwhile, was unaware of this exchange—he was panting and working his way through a carafe of water to quench the heat of a chili peppered Spaghetti Aglio e Olio.

'Oh, it's hot, it's hot!'

'Seven hundred years of Moorish occupation, and you're intolerant of spices?'

Anyone who has lived in a small community will tell you that there are two things that travel at the speed of light: light, and salacious gossip. The following morning, the colonel appeared at my door in the role of special envoy. I thought it unusual to receive a visit at nine o'clock in the morning.

I opened the door, still innocent of breakfast, and he came in. He perched on the arm of the sofa and refused both a coffee and a vodka and tonic, which led me to assume that he was the messenger of very grave news, such as harem pants making a comeback. In the tones of a palliative care nurse whose heart isn't really in it, he said to me, 'Well, I'm afraid I have to tell you that you're the talk of the town.' He was, of course, alluding to the sighting of me in an Italian restaurant with an unknown male.

'I went to dinner with a friend.'

'Well, you know what it's like in small towns.' His lips were pursed in parochial admonishment. Coming from a small community in County Mayo in Ireland, he did this rather well.

As the bus approached the city limits of Valencia, the gleaming skyscraper of the Torre de Francia came into view. In fact, one knew without looking through the window because its appearance usually coincided with the song, 'I Want to Know What Love Is' by Foreigner. The bus driver was both punctual and cleaved faithfully to the same soft rock compilation CD. My heart lifted: civilisation!

My weekend sojourns to Valencia had become more and more frequent, if not necessary. After a seven-year tenure in the sierra, I had turned somewhat hermit-like: detaching myself from the life of my immediate surroundings and collecting boxed sets of vintage television drama. In and of itself, the latter is unproblematic provided you ration yourself. But I was perilously skirting Anita Brookner territory, wrapped up in both a real and metaphorical cardigan from Advent Sunday until the Spring Equinox. This small tragedy was also accompanied by the desire to frame the photograph of a youthful Googie Withers, and display it. It stood on the dressing-table of a guest bedroom. A mother of an acquaintance once asked me, 'Who's that?'

'It's Googie Withers', I replied, staring at a corner of the ceiling.

'Oh, I thought it might have been you doing one of your stints.'

At that very moment, I knew that the time had finally arrived to put the house up for sale, with which Paul agreed over the telephone in London, to leave the *comarca* and return to the city. I prepared the house for sale, circulated the keys amongst the estate agents, and made plans to move to Valencia. Fortuitously, a rental apartment had become available in the same building where José-María and his partner lived.

Our requirements in life can change, as do our circumstances, and I once again needed the vitality of city life. Also, as Paul was now almost permanently residing in London, both for work and for health reasons, it was important to live within a taxi ride of an international airport.

My relocation to El Carmen, the historic district of Valencia, was orchestrated with the efficiency and economy of speech that normally accompanies the transportation of a detainee to a high-security facility. I was required to sign the one-year lease of an attic flat; to be sufficiently grateful to those who had organised my transplant; and to show an interest in others without recourse to mentioning deceased British actresses.

From my window, the view was very ecumenical and featured

the imposing tower of the Micalet, the cathedral of Valencia, together with the campanile and cobalt-blue dome of San José de Calasanz. On the evening that I moved in, the skies were uncharacteristically dense and gun-metal grey. The distinctive, almost mournful-sounding bells of the Micalet were marking the hour. In a city of radiant dawns—endlessly so in the long summer—and intense brightness, for we are nearer to Oran than Barcelona, rain is a delight. Also, a necessity because it irrigates the *huertas*, the orange groves and rice fields surrounding the city. The *Llevant* wind was coming in off the sea, and a late spring storm was gathering.

We were a diverse bunch distributed over four floors of a Modernist-period building on Calle Lope de Rueda, tucked just behind the Torres de Quart. The Torres de Quart are two cylindrical towers that formed one of the gates to medieval Valencia, as part of a wall that surrounded the city. There was no elevator, but a serpentine iron banister that coils upwards through the narrow stairwell and which, certainly, must have confounded quite a few undertakers in its time.

I am the custodian of a sideboard, a Cordovan *recibidor*, which curves out at the sides like a bourgeois matron at a pharmacy counter, and which met the Modernist banister of the stairwell. I don't think that one properly enters adulthood until one owns a sideboard. It was a difficult negotiation with many pauses, brow-mopping, and the imaginative blasphemy of long-dead saints. I had the sensation of being disliked for the full duration of its ascent, which evaporated only once at the top and after producing three bottles of wine, a pound of Manchego cheese, and the gift of a year calendar featuring nuns engaging in unlikely outdoors pursuits.

The girl across the hall from me was the perfect neighbour: a phantom whom one very occasionally heard but never saw. I think that, for most of the time, she lived somewhere else. Possibly with a boyfriend. Weeks of silence were interspersed with the sound of domestic industry heard through an open door: the rolling-up of shutter blinds; sweeping and mopping; the repetitive click of a sandal against a calloused heel.

Below, on the third floor, lived a married couple. The husband, who possessed arrestingly piercing blue eyes, appeared to be under a domestic edict by his machine-gun tongued, Malagueña wife to grow his hair long. On some previous visit to the building—to see José-María and his partner—I crossed him on the stairs. He looked like a crew-cut cameo player in Fassbinder's *Querelle de Brest*. Now, he looked like an unhappy ram awaiting the outcome of a sheep shearers' dispute. Our unofficial concierge on the ground floor, whom I will shortly come to, confided in me: 'When he started growing his hair, that's when their problems began.' I nodded vigorously, thus cementing our alliance in the shared conviction that an ill-advised hairstyle is linked to a downturn in economic prospects.

Also on the third floor lived two brothers who were gym fanatics. As befitted their testosterone and energy levels, they did not descend the stairs a step at a time but leapt whole flights. *Tick-tick-tick-BOOM, tick-tick-tick-BOOM*. It sounded as if two velociraptors were trapped in the stairwell. I frequently hoped that one of them would misjudge his air travel and disappear into the abyss — the stone tiles of the vestibule were crying out for drama.

There was, indeed, some drama when one of the "gym

brothers" had returned to the apartment without his key. Convinced that the other was inside the apartment yet not responding to the considerable banging on the front door, nor answering his mobile phone, the police and a locksmith were called. Curious, and attracted by the din, the residents of the building grouped together on the adjacent staircase, rubbernecking.

By chance, I was returning from the hairdresser's and on the way up to my apartment on the top floor. In so doing, I found myself at the centre of the action. This caused me to be more excited than concerned. A twenty-something police officer with jet black hair and designer stubble demanded to know who I was. I replied, rather elaborately, 'I am an artist and a well-wisher.'

Eventually, the locksmith broke into the apartment and the missing gym brother was, apparently, found unconscious on his bed. Rumour had it that he had overdosed on his own steroids.

On the second floor, lived my friends, who secured me this apartment through the owner of the building whose residence and office was situated in a glorious example of Art Nouveau facing the Plaza del Ayuntamiento. Inside, there was a hush that only reassuringly expensive décor creates. His apartment was an impossibly tasteful mélange of Corbusier, Roman busts and Turkmen kilims. On signing the rental contract for my apartment—which, in comparison, was a study in austerity—I had to stifle a curtsy.

Across from them lived a petite and muscular young woman who smoked very large quantities of marijuana yet steered a heavy, vintage bicycle through hellish traffic without incident. She wore army fatigues with impenetrably dark sunglasses and was by profession a barber. We suspected that she might be a Marxist, lesbian "sleeper" for the Basque Nationalists.

My informant was the aforementioned lady on the ground floor, who was a widow with time on her hands and our self-appointed concierge. After agreeing with her about the hairstyle of the man in number six, we shared an unspoken bond. She gatherered my mail, put it to one side, and when I came to collect it she divined the sender by carefully examining the envelope.

'Electricity bill from Iberdrola. It's shocking, isn't it? Thieves! This one is foreign, maybe it's a book? Ah, I know this.' She tapped at an official-looking envelope with a magenta nailed index finger and said, with unnecessary relish, 'It is a *multa!*' (a fine). Then she toddled back indoors, doubtless to stir a rustic soup, leaving me in a mild panic as to what I'd been fined for.

I knew little about her—not even her name—apart from the fact that she had an intense and consistent aversion to anything French. When a northerly wind arrived, shivering the palm fronds into a whispered frenzy, she would announce: 'Es un viento francés!' (It's a French wind!) When a *gota fría* moved in, bringing torrential downpours, I was standing in the vestibule debating whether to make a dash for the local bakery when her disembodied head appeared from behind her door. With a complicated expression at once knowing, philosophical, and resigned she declared:

'Es una tormenta *francesa!*' (It's a French rain storm!).

The storm had, in fact, blown in from the west, but I was not about to correct someone who had direct access to my personal correspondence.

The communal roof terrace was just above my apartment. I was, for the most part, its sole visitor and had already proprietorially furnished its south-westerly corner. One day, one of the gym brothers appeared. He pegged up a vest, skulked a little—pretending to take an interest in the view—and then ambled over to me. I was sat in my blue fold-up chair, making notes. We had a brief conversation that went like this:

'You are foreign?'

'Yes.'

'Where are you from?'

'It's complicated.'

'You speak Spanish?'

'Yes, I'm speaking it now.'

'How long have you been here?'

'Twenty minutes.'

Just below the roof terrace, in the foreground, a neighbour often appeared on his patio to water his plants with a garden hose. Nonchalantly, he would then lower his shorts and turn the hose on his exposed genitalia. This bathing generally took place behind a *Washingtonia filifera*. Beneath was a shady light-well where his wife sat at a balcony with open French doors, knitting. To me, this tableau illustrated the harmonious disconnectedness of modern life.

The city does not always guarantee anonymity. Shortly after my arrival there, I was returning from the supermarket laden with grocery bags full of Crianza and breadsticks for an upcoming party when, coming towards me on the crowded pavement, I saw my former next-door neighbour. Her daughter, whom she sometimes visited, lived in my new neighbourhood.

As we drew closer, she called my name. Unblinking, I stared ahead and quickened my pace, as one does at unwelcome attention. As I passed, I sensed her expression of surprise, urgency and then incomprehensibility. She called my name, again. Then again, as my head turned a corner, in a voice that could have sliced through tungsten. I thought: 'Am I to be spared nothing?' I took refuge in the nearest shop—which happened to special-ise in sex toys and erotica—and hid behind the window display. The sales assistant registered neither surprise nor interest; quite possibly because she simply assumed that

I had found my natural station in life.

Afterwards, I felt rather guilty about ignoring her. No doubt she would have seen the for sale sign posted on the front of the house, but to have stopped would have meant having to explain my departure, for reasons which I doubt she would have under-stood.

I recall that in our last conversation she had suggested that we build a higher wall between our respective terraces. To get from the back of the house onto the lower terrace, we had to build a wooden footbridge, which went past her light-well. She had obviously seen me from below, going back and forth over the bridge in a lace sarong and nothing else. A knee-length lace sarong and nothing else. Perhaps slightly shorter than knee-length. Lace is nature's own air conditioning, and I rather think that I'm allowed to dress as I please, especially in my own home.

Later that day, I wrote her daughter an email explaining that I had relocated after seeing Marisa Paredes in *The Flower of My Secret*. That, as the credits of the film rolled, I had made the decision to press ahead with gender reassignment and, further, that I had been advised to sever all ties with my former life.

Curiously, I thought this would be the simplest and most credible explanation, not that I owed her one. It occurred to me only after hitting the send button: what if she sees me in six months' time and I look exactly the same?

When I related this encounter and subsequent email to Paul, he said to me, 'Why didn't you just tell her that you were *fucking bored*?'

Once again, I was living in the city. A city of markets, and ferreterias that open on Sundays; delicatessens that sell Greek and Lebanese specialities; bars and restaurants whose *azulejos* ricochet with the cross-fire of orders delivered in a perfume of leather base notes. A city of Malian itinerants of supernatural grace, arranging ebony and crocodile leather on rolls of fabric that make a vertiginous decoration of the pavement; of glacial, Carpathian call-girls; of Colombian *gorrillas*, the small army of unofficial parking attendants; of plentiful taxis at 3AM and even the occasional murder, which I have always yearned for.

I was, for the time being, home.

VOLVER

AFTER REPLACING THE TELEPHONE RECEIVER, I felt completely numb. Frozen. It was one of those moments when time is suspended; when the world—your world—shifts suddenly from the material to the abstract. Then, I knew that the Spanish chapter of my life, our lives, was ineluctably over. In a sense, it had been over for Paul for some time; he could often be working on location for weeks, sometimes months, at a time.

Paul and I have never been the kind of partners who, if one is temporarily absent for a short period, the other feels bereft and purposeless. However, it is also true that there is little point in being in a partnership if you are a thousand miles apart, and separated for prolonged durations. Calle de Lope de Rueda, Valencia was not the "solution", but a staging post between the *comarca* and London. The pattern of our lives had changed, and I had commuted between Valencia and London with enough frequency that I was recognised by the cabin crew, but there was now no doubt that I would return to England permanently.

Paul had telephoned me only after having been released from hospital, where he spent three days. It was not unusual for us to occasionally pass almost a week without speaking, and I had simply assumed that he was busy.

He had left his vehicle and was crossing a supermarket car park when his vision became tunnelled and he fell to his knees. It was sudden and without warning. Heart attack. However, he could see that he was kneeling next to a Kia Picanto. Refusing to die adjacent to a compact car manufactured in South Korea, he gathered himself enough to move forward where there was parked a Mercedes. He slumped onto the bonnet and blacked out.

Providentially, and crucially, the woman who was sat in the driver's seat of the Mercedes was medically trained, and administered CPR until the emergency services arrived. He was told by the surgeon that he was only minutes away from death. She saved Paul's life; without her intervention, the surgeon said he would almost certainly have died.

I asked Paul in which supermarket car park it had happened.

'Asda in High Wycombe,' he replied.

'Asda in High Wycombe? We can't tell people that, it's *far* too downmarket. We'll say that it was outside Waitrose. In Gerrards Cross.'

Even when approximate to death, one may still find a little humour.

When our telephone conversation was terminated, I moved as if in a dream—my legs weighted—and made immediate arrangements to leave. It also marked the beginning of the protracted affair of releasing mysel from one life—with all its exigencies— and transplanting myself into another. There were practical considerations, not least the moving of the Cordovan *recibidor* back down a torturously tight stairwell to the ground floor.

A longstanding friend of mine, Paul Burston, who is a novelist and the founder of the Polari Literary Salon, once said to me, 'If change is inevitable, one must embrace it.' This is very true although, of course, it can take time to process change.

The first edition of this book, published in 2011, won the Polari First Book Prize, which is an award given to a debut work that explores the LGBT experience. In support of the book's publication, I appeared at numerous spoken word events—including Duckie at the Royal Vauxhall Tavern and, several times, at Polari which is hosted at London's Southbank.

At one evening—whilst being praised lavishly by a delighted audience, might I add—I attempted to inch towards the dressing room as my beloved Paul gathered the bouquets and garlands. Paul Burston appeared and embraced me: 'You have surpassed yourself, love!' Well, it was lovely. The seamless negotiation from plush carpeting to an awaiting saloon car completed, I was whisked to a restaurant for a light fish supper. This could only possibly have happened to me in London.

I enjoyed these readings, which were a new experience for me, and which grew into performance—memorising the key scenes of a chapter and retelling them anecdotally. I plan to return to it, again. Additionally, and sporadically, I have also begun to record songs after a lengthy hiatus.

Change: as I have previously mentioned, when one undergoes a significant life event such as a divorce, a bereavement or switching one's internet provider, one requires time to process the experience. When I returned to live in London, which is, after all, the city of my birth, I felt like an outsider. I felt as if I were "of it" but not belonging *to* it, so to speak, which was a curious feeling.

In particular, this sense of otherness was underscored by the unpredictable, maritime climate and the opaque skies that accompany it. One is illuminated, more often than not, by poor quality light conditions—compared to the intense luminance of southern climes— which lend an ashen flatness to everything. The sun is less a presence, than a suggestion. I did wonder how people could endure it, but then I did until, at age forty-four, Paul and I set off on our adventure. The upside of British weather is that it gives everyone a topic with which to initiate conversation; or acts as a substitute for real conversation when people no longer have anything to say to each other. In contrast, remarking to a Valencian ironmonger, in July, 'It's sunny again!' is plain daft and would elicit a look of confusion.

Because my integration into Spanish life had been such a resounding triumph, I was attuned to a Mediterranean rhythm and an Iberian culture. This manifested itself in different forms, from the obvious to the subtle. For example, I shouted instead of speaking, and when someone replied in a normal voice I would either ask them to repeat themselves, or wondered why they were so withdrawn. There is the distinct likelihood that I might be going deaf in one ear—which is common amongst singers who have spent a large amount of time stationed next to a pile of Marshall amps—but I am too vain to admit it.

On occasion, I would forget the English adjective—or more disastrously, the noun—for something, but I would know its Spanish equivalent.

'What's that thing called, you know, the thing they put in a coffee shop when there's been a spillage and they don't want a customer going arse over tit, suing them? It's a health and safety thing.'

'A *cone*.'

There was a cultural adjustment: it took me ages to stop reflex-ively acknowledging strangers, shop-owners, and even dogs, with a greeting. Sometimes, a breezy 'Good morning' to a fellow traveller standing on a station platform was welcomed; con-versely, the reaction could be alarm, suspicion or a watchful eye in case I produced a sharp object. On the subject of travel, Paul one day passed me a card.

'What's this?'

'It's an Oyster Card,' he said, 'You'll need it for bus travel.' Praise be to St Agnes, I had no idea what an Oyster Card was.

'Please don't do this to me,' I replied instinctively, in the calm and measured tone of someone who might have suffered a scheduled humiliation, but who had now reached their threshold.

I really don't think there's anything quite as aging as sitting in a bus stop shelter, wearing a water-repellent garment to ward off the creeping pneumonia of a fine drizzle, whilst waiting to flag down a Green Line bus.

On a side note, I refuse point blank to watch the television evening news, or to pore over the carnage that passes for local headlines. This might make me less informed, but I do not feel impoverished by *not* knowing the body count of a discotheque fire in Biggleswade. Previously, I survived eleven years without a satellite dish, for the simple reason that I didn't want to be drilled, hourly, by catastrophe. I still haven't got into the habit of watching television: schadenfreude at the misfortune of others is abundant, and if Britain was once 'a nation of shop-keepers', it is now a nation of amateur chefs whose Genoise sponge fails to rise and "celebrities" who have risen without trace.

These are all minor, yet significant, elements in the course of adaptation. Paul had survived a near-death experience and we were both together again, in the sense of once more living together. Also, he had made a full recovery.

My belief is that you can live in two geographical places, but what you cannot do is to flutter between them. By this, I mean that you cannot live a life of emotional compartmentalism; a life that is divided between two concurrent desires. Eventually, notwithstanding the dubious pleasure at being in a priority boarding queue whilst others are forced—through lack of floor space—to encircle an airport shop, it is a disharmonious pattern. In stronger terms, it is mildly schizophrenic. I believe that such an existence is sustainable but, ultimately, it cannot be *sustained*.

Recently, I revisited Bermondsey, which I had not seen in over twenty years. Where once stood social housing estates, there are now shiny, aspirational luxury developments, and the recognisable landmarks of my adolescence have long-since disappeared. The docks—which were in the throes of death, even then—have gone. Entire streets have vanished; the signage is replaced; and a once-favoured Greek restaurant is now a swish, mortuary-illuminated tanning and nail salon. In the flux of change, the past is paved over to make way for the future; the topography is progressively transformed and re-emerges with new contours.

Although, the North Peckham Civic Library building remains. It is no longer a library, but a community church. It was there that, unbidden, I occasionally refiled books: anything of a religious nature was moved to the Fantasy section; true crime books were reclassified as Spiritual & Self-Help.

I do not have a "Memory Lane"; they demolished it and changed its name. (In any case, my Memory Lane was not a place of picnicked excursion, but a dark alleyway littered with the bodies of discarded bass players and bewildered accountants.) But this is how it should be, because there is nothing more pointless as nostalgia, as there is nothing more futile than regret. Of the latter, to atone is more useful, and more appreciated by the victim.

There is only one direction in which life travels—forwards— and should you stand still then, you, too, will be paved over.

London, 2017.

AFTERWORD

AS I HAVE SAID BEFORE. when one reaches middle age or, more accurately, *late* middle age, one's primary fear is not the spectre of death; it is of being pauperised by one's own longevity. Quite simply, some people live longer than they had budgeted for. So, you see, being a teetotal, non-smoking salad enthusiast does have its setbacks. The second concern is health. Although, if one is obliged to eke out a living in severely reduced circumstances—three of the most terrifying words in the English language when used together—one cannot but wish for a rapid decline in health, and a quick death.

Whilst it's important to maintain appearance, if only for appearance's sake, how one looks becomes less important; hopefully, at this point, you're not trying to snare a confused undergraduate with your complexion. Certainly, one should not attempt coquettishness once over the age of twenty-one: it works for ingénues in musicals, but on anyone else it looks *poignant* or, worse, sinister. My view is that stalkers are merely people to whom we're not attracted. When we are shadowed and constantly messaged with obsessive texts declaring undying love for us by those to whom we *are* attracted, we call them a fiancé.

I do think that sex is very important to one's equilibrium

and it should be prolonged as far as possible. To those in later age who lament the absence of a sex life, my advice is to research which area of the country has the highest incidence of gerontophilia and telephone Pickfords removals company for a quote. After all, sexual attack is only "attack" when it is unwanted; otherwise, you have found yourself something to look forward to. By all means, leave a side window of your bungalow open during the hours of darkness, thus allowing easier access to the nimble, night-time visitor. In the event that one is murdered, it's not all bad: you'll never have to sit through *Angela's Ashes*, again.

Expressing concerns to a friend is generally healthier than remaining mute and contained, we should remember that a problem shared is not always a problem halved — it can be a problem *doubled*. Rather than externalising yourself all over everyone else's breakfast cereal, be a little selective about what you telegraph. For example, if someone criticises your pastry making, disappointment rather than distress is the more appropriate response. It doesn't give you carte blanche to seek out an online support forum who, no doubt, will overanalyse your misfortune, declare you a victim and insist you demand a safe space.

Younger people sometimes ask for my opinion. It is flattering and cosily satisfying, but I am somewhat at a loss to understand why anyone should consult *me*. While it is true that I am unfazed at the prospect of being planted, with a shopping list, in the middle of a busy fruit and veg market in Bogotá, were you to ask me to fry an egg, I would psychologically fall apart. I have a morbid fear of being spat at by appliances. My view on scrambled egg is that it is an *omelette without ambition*, and if you don't cook it in a non-stick pan, your kitchen becomes a gulag. Since we're in the kitchen, I should like to say this: anyone who leaves a cut, raw onion in a refrigerator without wrapping it in cling film, clearly despises mankind. Nobody wants to open a refrigerator door and be knocked off their feet by an aromatic, stark-naked shallot.

I recognise that some people's allergies are very real. I used to be of the opinion that an allergy sufferer was an attention-seeker who, unchecked, had successfully progressed onto manifesting his or her "symptoms" as a ploy for special consideration. I do believe that modern life is poisoning us, as allergies did not properly exist prior to 1950. There is no historical account that I can find of a person driving an open-top sports car through fields of rapeseed and, blinded by stinging tears, crashing into a tree. Neither can I find an incidence of anyone being rushed to the cottage hospital, fighting for their life, from the scene of a bucolic, civilised picnic after digesting the rennet in a Ploughman's Lunch. But it's also possible that, in an earlier time, people were too engaged in the daily routine of survival to notice that they are intolerant to Balsam of Peru. A case in point being an aunt of mine who was in the middle of distributing a whole rack of lamb when Hitler decided to bomb Rotherhithe. She'd spent so long cooking it that everyone agreed to stay at the table and take their chances. Recounting the story to me, she added, rather unnecessarily, 'Depressed? I didn't have the *luxury* of being depressed.'

I revised my opinion when, on an aeroplane, someone a few rows forward opened up a complimentary packet of peanuts, and the passenger seated next to me immediately went into anaphylactic shock. I missed the Dolomites, as I was frantically pressing the attendant call button whilst her lips inflated to the size of those of a prizewinning carp.

Questions posed to me are often of the weightier, life choice kind. I think that working should always be an election, not a necessity; however, the current economic system is not geared in favour of the masses, but to the few. Rather than having more leisure time we are increasingly enslaved by working longer hours, under more uncertain conditions, in order to consume things that we don't need. (I was almost drowned by a wave of truculence when, recently, I announced, 'I don't know anyone with an iPhone who's *happy*.') If you don't really want to work— which is a perfectly reasonable desire— there are two options: become an artist, or over-educate yourself out of all possibility of meaningful employment.

Foreign travel is an excellent aspiration, and experiencing new lands and cultures is very enriching. As Mark Twain once wrote, 'Travel is fatal to prejudice, bigotry, and narrow-mindedness...' Everyone should get lost, in France, at least once in their lives, although preferably without the Bonnie Tyler backing track. But before you set off, ensure that you have adequate funds: there are few things more unbecoming than driving a hard bargain with a beleaguered, Indian stallholder for the sake of a few rupees, because you have convinced yourself that you're a "traveller" and not a tourist. You're a tourist.

I have travelled fairly extensively, successfully navigating myself towards an international buffet on six of the seven continents, and remarkably my only misfortune took place at Cairo railway station. I had to visit the toilet, the awfulness of which I cannot describe, and got trapped in a cubicle when the door lock snapped off in my hand, rendering me permanently "occupied".

The tiled floor was awash with effluence, and I could sense typhoid seeping into my sandals as my train chuffed out of the station bound for Alexandria.

On writing, the oft-asked question is how one summons the inspiration to write. One may as well ask, 'How do I summon Maurice Chevalier?' There are many workshops and courses that help writers to develop and hone their skills, and learning about structure, characterisation and plotting is highly useful. When attempting my novella, my first stride into fiction, I chose an improvisational approach, working with a very loose set of ideas and no roadmap. All went well, until Chapter Six, where I hit a very frustrating block. I recommend purchasing a cork board from the stationer's and hanging it above your desk.

Writing is the act of sitting down, creating a blank page and not leaving your station until it is filled. It is, alas, rather like woodworking in the sense that it is 90% perspiration. Except that you can wear a cravat.

Every writer is different when it comes to optimal hours and routine. Personally, I like an early start, finishing for late lunch. Also, every writer is a "Word Count Queen" who sets themselves a daily target. Whilst this is important in terms of self-discipline, it is the quality of one's output that matters, not its length. This is a useful dictum for life in general.

Never, on any account, write for an audience—it is a mistake—write for *yourself*. Similarly, as an artist, I think it can be beneficial to solicit the opinion of others, but it is key to always go with one's instinct. Nobody knows you better than you. Otherwise, one ends up with a "democratically-elected" outcome.

Democracy is, by and large, a good thing—except when referenda do not swing in your favour—but in the creative arts it has a tendency to mediocratise the original vision. After all, Mozart didn't go about the streets of Vienna asking people whether 'Eine kleine Nachtmusik' should be a little more *up tempo*, did he?

Lastly, if I could impart one piece of truly invaluable advice to anyone, it would be this: *Never drink a fortified wine when sitting with your back to a heat source, such as a radiator. You will be lavishly sick.*

PHOTO CREDITS

Author Photograph (James) © **Jean Margaret**

Dedication page (Paul Buchanan) © **James Maker**

My Provenance is South London 60 (James) **family archive**

Rock and Roll Susancide (James) **photo-me-booth**

A Leonard Short of a Trio (James) **photo-me-booth**

The Max Factor Fundamentalists (James) © **Morrissey**

1976 (James) © **Kamil Tahir**

Elephant and Castle Boot Girls (James) © **Jean Attree**

Morrissey (Morrissey) **photo-me-booth**

Annette, Please Contact Reception (James) © **Kamil Tahir**

The Parlour of Maitresse Desclaves (James) © **James Maker**

Coda (Paul Buchanan) © **James Maker**

The Sentinel of Studholme Street (James) © **Angela Spray**

Raymonde © **Steve Speller**

RPLA: The Lipstick Swindle © **Alistair Thain**

Haircentricity (James) © **Jean Attree**

The Cumberland Sausages are Mine (James) © **Paul Buchanan**

The Jeffrey Dahmer Party Years (James and Nikki Kastner) © **Simon Hoare**

The Runaway Constable (James) © **Nikki Kastner**

Mr Maker Changes Trains (James) © **Peter Ashworth**

Nueva Vida, Nueva Aventura (James) © **James Maker**

Soirées of Terpsichore (James) © **João Vilaverde Mugeiro**

Last Exit to Valencia (James) © **João Vilaverde Mugeiro**

Volver (James) © **Justin David**

ACKNOWLEDGEMENTS

I would like to give my heartfelt appreciation to both Nathan Evans and Justin David of Inkandescent. To Nathan for having the eye of a condor as editor, and holding the compact up to my face so that I may properly reapply a metaphorical lipstick. To Justin for creating the most perfect art work for this book, together with its layout and typesetting. And for remembering who Ann George was.

James Maker 2017

The publishers would like to express their gratitude to Daren Kay, Derek Benton and James Greig who gave their help so generously during the making of this book.

Inkandescent 2017

Also from Inkandescent

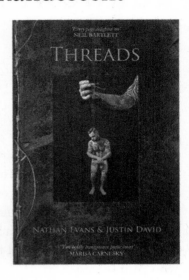

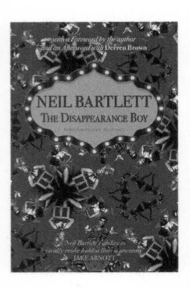

www.inkandescent.co.uk

Also from Inkandescent

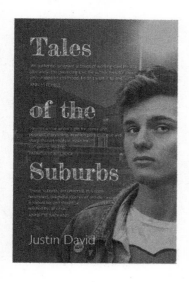

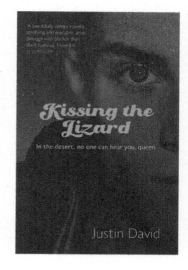

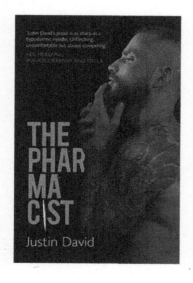

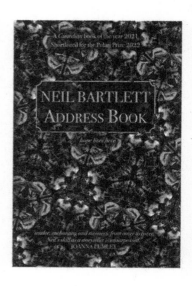

www.inkandescent.co.uk

The Inkandescent Writing School

Telling Tails
new creative writing classes

It's time to invest in yourself! Acclaimed author Justin David brings a wealth of writing knowledge to deliver compact, nuts and bolts courses that will help you successfully craft your first piece of prose.

For more information and to register your interest, visit:

www.inkandescent.co.uk/writing-courses

by outsiders for outsiders

Inkandescent Publishing was created in 2016
by Justin David and Nathan Evans to shine a light on
diverse and distinctive voices.

Could you do one more Inkredible thing for us?
Sign up to our mailing list to stay informed
about future releases:

www.inkandescent.co.uk/sign-up

follow us on Facebook:

@InkandescentPublishing

on Twitter:

@InkandescentUK

on Threads:

@inkandescentuk

and on Instagram:

@inkandescentuk